Planning and Role Setting for Public Libraries

A Manual of Options and Procedures

Prepared for the Public Library Development Program

by
Charles R. McClure
Amy Owen
Douglas L. Zweizig
Mary Jo Lynch
Nancy A. Van House

American Library Association
Chicago and London

Cover designed by Thomas Sollers

Text designed by Deborah Doering

Composed by Impressions, Inc. in
    ITC Garamond and Gill Sans on
    a Penta-driven Autologic APS-μ5
    Phototypesetting system.

Printed on 50-pound Glatfelter, a
    pH-neutral stock, and bound in
    10-point Carolina cover stock by
    Malloy Lithographing, Inc.

Library of Congress Cataloging-in-Publication Data

Planning and role setting for public libraries.

    Includes index.
    1. Public libraries—Standards—Handbooks, manuals,
etc. 2. Public libraries—Aims and objectives—
Handbooks, manuals, etc. 3. Library planning—Handbooks,
manuals, etc. I. McClure, Charles R. II. Public
Library Association. New Standards Task Force.
Z678.85.P58   1987   027.4′0202   87-11445
ISBN 0-8389-3341-6

95 94   9 8 7

Contents

Biographical Information
about the Authors   113

Figures

Presidents' Message

The Public Library Association exists to assist public librarians in giving better service to users of their libraries. In that continuing tradition, over the past four years a major project has come to fruition in the Public Library Development Program, of which this volume is one product.

Many librarians and libraries have contributed expertise, work, and money to this program. As presidents of the Public Library Association during the four years just past, we owe a special debt to the faithful hard work and professional excellence of the members of the New Standards Task Force and especially to the Task Force's guiding hand, its chair, Karen Krueger.

PLA is justifiably proud of the participation of so many of its members in an effort that promises so much to the improvement of public library service in the years to come. As presidents of PLA during the development of the program, we wish to express our appreciation to all who have been associated with it.

Nancy M. Bolt, President, 1983–84
Charles W. Robinson, President, 1984–85
Patrick M. O'Brien, President, 1985–86
Kathleen M. Balcom, President, 1986–87

Foreword

Planning and Role Setting for Public Libraries is one component of the Public Library Development Program (PLDP), a combination of activities and products developed by the Public Library Association (PLA) to assist public libraries in the areas of planning, measurement, and evaluation. These activities and products were designed to continue the philosophy and work done previously by PLA in this area. PLDP was supported by the Public Library Association, the Chief Officers of State Library Agencies (COSLA), and the Urban Libraries Council (ULC). The three products developed as a part of the Public Library Development Program are:

This manual, Planning and Role Setting for Public Libraries

Output Measures for Public Libraries, second edition, by Nancy A. Van House, Mary Jo Lynch, Charles R. McClure, Douglas L. Zweizig, and Eleanor Jo Rodger (Chicago: American Library Association, 1987)

The design and specifications for a public library data service.

These tools are the result of discussions by the PLA New Standards Task Force regarding the need for new qualitative and quantitative standards for public libraries. Although some librarians prefer prescriptive quantitative standards, there was strong support at the 1984 ALA Conference Hearing for PLA's position that library services should be tailored to specific communities and based on local planning and decision-making. The Task Force, having reviewed the enormous progress made by libraries and PLA in the areas of local planning and evaluation, decided to build on what had al-

ready been done rather than create national standards.

There were two primary building blocks for the Public Library Development Program, both of which were created largely due to the efforts of the PLA Goals, Guidelines, and Standards Committee. The first was *A Planning Process for Public Libraries* by Vernon E. Palmour et al. (Chicago: American Library Association, 1980). This step-by-step guide to local planning for public libraries was produced with support from a U.S. Office of Education grant. As a result of this publication and its use by libraries, it became apparent that libraries needed assistance with measuring their performance in terms of library services (outputs) rather than library resources (inputs). The second building block, *Output Measures for Public Libraries* by Douglas L. Zweizig and Eleanor Jo Rodger (Chicago: American Library Association, 1982), was developed to fill that need. *Output Measures* identified a set of measures related to common public library service activities and included a set of standardized procedures for these measures.

After a number of years of experience with these two tools, librarians were knowledgeable enough to articulate the strengths and weaknesses of both manuals. In addition, the Task Force identified two rather unexplored areas which seemed to have great potential for helping libraries choose directions and establish priorities. The first of these, the library roles concept, resulted from work done by Lowell Martin, who observed that public libraries try to do too much and as a result find it difficult to provide the quality of services desired. He suggested that the complex set of services public libraries provide their communities could be grouped under a set of service profiles, or roles, from which each library could choose a few on which to focus. Development of this roles concept was seen as an important element of a new or enhanced planning tool.

The second unexplored (or perhaps undeveloped) area is comparative data. In the measurement part of the planning process, librarians were looking at data on their library's performance and asking "compared to what?" Although internal comparison over time is preferred, the need for information on other libraries in similar communities with similar resources was real. The Task Force decided that the provision of such data in a timely manner would greatly enhance library planning efforts.

As a result of this review of libraries' planning and evaluation needs, the Public Library Development Program was created. The development of a revised planning manual with emphasis on role setting, the revision of the output measures manual, and the design of a data service that could provide libraries with comparative data for planning—all three closely interrelated—were seen by the Task Force as the best possible assistance PLA could give libraries. It was determined that prescriptive standards, if needed, should be developed at the state and local level.

With this idea and with funding for the project from COSLA, ULC, and individual public libraries, a contract was signed in 1985 with Charles R. McClure, president of Information Management Consultant Services Inc., for production of the desired tools. McClure, as principal investigator, and Mary Jo Lynch, Amy Owen, Nancy Van House, and Douglas Zweizig made up the project study team. In January 1987 they completed the planning and measurement manuals and the design and specifications for the public library data service.

The three products of the Public Library Development Program, described below, are designed to be used either together or independently.

- *Planning and Role Setting for Public Libraries* describes a step-by-step planning process and introduces the concept of role selection. The manual guides the library as it reviews existing conditions and services, defines the library's mission, sets goals and objectives, chooses strategies for achieving objectives, and evaluates the results of the process.

- *Output Measures for Public Libraries,* second edition, describes a set of measures to assess common public library services. Instructions are included for collecting, analyzing, and interpreting data.

- The Public Library Data Service (PLDS) will collect and make accessible a selective set of data from public libraries across the country. It will contain four kinds of data:
  Selected output measures
  Library descriptors, including role choices
  Input data such as holdings, staff, and operating expenditures
  Community data such as population, age distribution, and income.

As this manual goes to press, the PLDS has been designed and is being tested. Implementation is scheduled for 1988.

The Public Library Development Program is both a continuation and a beginning. In order to assist public libraries in providing better library service in their communities, it has been necessary to look both at past experiences and future needs. There is no doubt the past has been exciting. With the progress of PLDP thus far, the future seems even more so.

PLA New Standards Task Force

Karen Krueger, chair
Carolyn Additon Anthony
Kathleen Mehaffey Balcom
Nancy M. Bolt
Mary Jo Detweiler
Ronald A. Dubberly
James H. Fish
June M. Garcia
Claudya B. Muller
Charles W. Robinson
Eleanor Jo Rodger
Elliot Shelkrot

Acknowledgments

Like the Constitution of the United States, this volume is the result of the work of many people. It is, of course, our hope it will engender the same kind of interest and discussion in the relatively small public library community as the Constitution did in the former colonies, but we make no claims to comparable literary excellence. We will be satisfied if this product and other products and services of the Public Library Development Program are useful to trustees, administrators, and staff members of public libraries.

The Public Library Association is grateful to many people and many institutions who have had a part in the Public Library Development Program during the past four years:

The Chief Officers of State Library Agencies and the Urban Library Council, co-sponsors with PLA of the Public Library Development Program. By their recognition and support of this effort, COSLA and ULC have provided the resource documents and services designed to assist public libraries in the provision of services to their users.

Nancy Bolt, who as President of PLA appointed the members of the New Standards Task Force and gave them their charge.

The New Standards Task Force (members listed below), whose professional experience, commitment, and ability to engage in endless hours of productive meetings gave shape, form, and guidance to the project.

Karen Krueger, who overfulfilled Nancy Bolt's expectations as the chair of the Task Force, and whose polite but firm leadership made sense from what often seemed confusion.

Charles Robinson, whose persistence in raising funds from public libraries all across the nation provided not only resources from but also participation by the public library community.

Gary Strong, the chair of COSLA, who provided the vision and leadership which elicited money, advice, and commitment from state libraries.

The over 150 individual public and state libraries (listed below) that contributed—and are still contributing—to the Public Library Development Program. Their commitment of funds has made the program and its products, of which this volume is one, truly a cooperative effort of America's public libraries.

Ronald Dubberly and Alex Ladenson, who for PLA and the Urban Libraries Council, respectively, provided administrative and financial management for the project.

The Study Team (listed below), whose patience, honesty, frankness, vision, and uncanny ability to meet unreasonable deadlines gave new meaning to the term "consultants."

ALA Publishing Services staff, notably Gary Facente and Helen Cline, for their continuing help and advice and their insistence on excellence in product design.

The Test Sites (listed below), without which reality might have been missed, and whose forebearance and suggestions have resulted in products more likely to be used and to improve public library service.

ELEANOR JO RODGER
Executive Director
Public Library Association

June 1987

New Standards Task Force

Appointed by PLA President Nancy Bolt in 1983, most NSTF members have changed their institutional affiliations in the meantime. Hence multiple credits appear after many names.

Chair: Karen J. Krueger (Arrowhead Library System, Wis.; Janesville, Wis., Public Library); *members:* Carolyn A. Anthony (Baltimore County and Skokie public libraries), Nancy Bolt (JNR Associates; Colorado State Library), Mary J. Detweiler (Prince William County, Md., Public Library; Dynix Inc.), Ronald A. Dubberly (Seattle and Atlanta-Fulton public libraries), June M. Garcia (Phoenix Public Library), Claudya B. Muller (Iowa State Library; Suffolk County, N.Y., Cooperative Library System), Charles W. Robinson (Baltimore County Public Library), Elliot Shelkrot (Pennsylvania State Library; Free Library of Philadelphia), Eleanor Jo Rodger (Fairfax County, Va., Public Library; Enoch Pratt Free Library; PLA), James H. Fish (Springfield, Mass., City Library), Kathleen Balcom (Downers Grove, Ill., Public Library).

Study Team

Using the framework outlined by the New Standards Task Force and responding to their guidance, the Study Team wrote the two manuals published by ALA Publishing Services and specified the design of the Public Library Data Service, now (June 1987) in preparation for implementation in early 1988.

Principal investigator, Charles R. McClure (University of Oklahoma; Syracuse University)

Nancy A. Van House (University of California–Berkeley)

Amy Owen (Utah State Library)

Douglas L. Zweizig (University of Wisconsin–Madison)

Mary Jo Lynch (Office for Research, American Library Association)

Test Sites

A number of libraries were selected by the Study Team as test sites to evaluate the usefulness and practicality of both manuals. As a result of the staff time and attention to the assignment, the Study Team received many valuable suggestions—suggestions which have made the manuals more valuable to those who will use them. Additional libraries, not listed here, are contin-uing to contribute to the success of the program by testing questionnaires of the Public Library Data Service. The test sites and coordinators are:

Alameda County (Calif.) Public Library—Ginnie Cooper; Newark Branch—Pat Zahn; Union City Branch—Linda Harris

Arlington Heights (Ill.) Memorial Library—Frank Dempsey

Clearwater (Fla.) Public Library—Carolyn Moore

DeKalb Library System (Ga.)—Donna Mancini

Denver (Colo.) Public Library—Rick J. Ashton

Iowa City (Iowa) Public Library—Lolly Eggers

Oakland (Calif.) Public Library—Lelia White

Oklahoma Department of Libraries—Sandy Ellison

Portland–Multnomah County (Ore.) Library—Sarah Long

Providence (R.I.) Public Library—Annalee Bundy

Salt Lake City (Utah) Public Library—Dennis Day

Spokane (Wash.) Public Library—Betty Bender

Springfield (Mass.) City Library—James Fish

Topeka (Kans.) Public Library—Bonnie Campbell

Washington County (Utah) Library—Russell Shirts

Wauwatosa (Wis.) Public Library—Margaret McGowan

Wilbraham (Mass.) Public Library—Paula Polk.

Photographs

The following libraries contributed photographs of staff members and library users for this publication:

Baltimore County Public Library
Los Angeles County Public Library
Phoenix Public Library
Skokie (Ill.) Public Library
Springfield (Mass.) City Library

Contributors

The Public Library Development Program is completely funded by state library agencies and individual public libraries across the nation. The nearly $200,000 contributed so far (April 1987) is, as far as we know, the most significant financial effort made to date in support of a cooperative project with no direct federal grants or foundation support. These libraries have reason to be proud of their support.

State Library Agencies

Alabama	Missouri
Alaska	Montana
Arizona	Nebraska
Arkansas	New Jersey
California	New York
Colorado	Oklahoma
Connecticut	Pennsylvania
Florida	Rhode Island
Hawaii	South Carolina
Indiana	South Dakota
Iowa	Tennessee
Kansas	Utah
Louisiana	Virginia
Maryland	Washington
Massachusetts	Wisconsin
Michigan	Wyoming
Mississippi	

Library Associations

Arkansas Library Association
Canadian Library Association
Connecticut Library Association
Illinois Library Association
Ontario Library Association
Pennsylvania Library Association, Southern Chapter
Rhode Island Library Association
Springfield (Mass.) Library and Museums Association
Texas Library Association
Wilton (Conn.) Library Association

Public Libraries

Abington (Pa.) Free Library
Alachua County (Fla.) Public Library
Alexandria (Va.) Public Library
Allen County (Ind.) Public Library
Amherst (N.Y.) Public Library
Ashtabula County (Ohio) District Library
Atlanta-Fulton (Ga.) Public Library
Baltimore County (Md.) Public Library
Bangor (Maine) Public Library
Bethlehem (Pa.) Public Library
Birmingham (Ala.) Public Library
Bloomfield Township (Mich.) Public Library
Bloomingdale (Ill.) Public Library
Boulder (Colo.) Public Library
Boynton Beach (Fla.) City Library
Brookline (Mass.) Public Library
Brooklyn (N.Y.) Public Library
Broward County (Fla.) Library
Bucks County (Pa.) Free Library
Buena Park Library District (Calif.)
Buffalo and Erie County (N.Y.) Public Library
Bur Oak Library System (Ill.)
Carnegie-Stout (Iowa) Public Library
Carroll County (Md.) Public Library
Cary Memorial Library (Mass.)
Cass County (Miss.) Public Library
Champaign (Ill.) Public Library
Cheltenham Township Library System (Pa.)
Cherokee County (S.C.) Public Library
Chester County (Pa.) Library
Chicago (Ill.) Public Library
Chickasaw Public Library System (Okla.)
Clark County (Nev.) Public Library
Clearwater (Fla.) Public Library
Cleveland Heights (Ohio) Public Library
Cobb County (Ga.) Public Library
Public Library of Columbus and Franklin County (Ohio)
Crystal Lake (Ill.) Public Library
Cumberland County (Pa.) Public Library
Dallas (Tex.) Public Library
Daniel Boone Regional Library (Mo.)
Dauphin County (Pa.) Library System
DeKalb Library System (Ga.)
Denver (Colo.) Public Library
Detroit (Mich.) Public Library
Dougherty County (Ga.) Public Library
Downers Grove (Ill.) Public Library
Durham County (N.C.) Library
East Baton Rouge Parish (La.) Library
East Orange (N.J.) Public Library
Englewood (Colo.) Public Library
Enoch Pratt Free Library (Md.)
Elyria (Ohio) Public Library
Escondido (Calif.) Public Library
Evansville–Vanderburgh County (Ind.) Public Library
Fairfield (Conn.) Public Library
Findley–Hancock County (Ohio) Public Library
Finkelstein Memorial Library (N.Y.)
Framingham (Mass.) Public Library
Fresno County (Calif.) Free Library
Gail Borden Public Library District (Ill.)
Geauga County (Ohio) Public Library
Genesee District Library (Mich.)
Grand Rapids (Mich.) Public Library
Granite City (Ill.) Public Library
Harford County (Md.) Library
Hartford (Conn.) Public Library
Harvey (Ill.) Public Library
Haverhill (Mass.) Public Library
Hennepin County (Minn.) Library System
Hildebrand Memorial Library (Wis.)
Holyoke (Mass.) Public Library

Houston (Tex.) Public Library
Huntington Beach (Calif.) Public Library
Huntsville (Ala.) Public Library
Indianapolis–Marion County (Ind.) Public Library
Iowa City (Iowa) Public Library
Jefferson County (Colo.) Public Library
Jefferson Parish (La.) Library
Joliet (Ill.) Public Library
Kansas City (Kans.) Public Library
Kansas City (Mo.) Public Library
Kilsap Regional Library (Wash.)
Lake County (Ind.) Public Library
Lake Lanier Regional Library (Ga.)
Las Vegas–Clark County Library District (Nev.)
Lexington (Ky.) Public Library
Lincoln (Neb.) City Libraries
Lisle Library District (Ill.)
Long Beach (Calif.) Public Library
Los Angeles County (Calif.) Public Library
Madison (Wis.) Public Library
Marin County (Calif.) Free Library
Metropolitan Library System (Okla.)
Miami-Dade (Fla.) Public Library
Mid-Hudson Library System (N.Y.)
Middle Georgia Regional Library
Milan (Mich.) Public Library
Milwaukee (Wis.) Public Library
Mobile (Ala.) Public Library
Mt. Prospect (Ill.) Public Library
Nevada County (Calif.) Library
New Hanover County (N.C.) Public Library
New Orleans (La.) Public Library
New York (N.Y.) Public Library
Newark (N.J.) Public Library
Norfolk (Va.) Public Library
Northbrook (Ill.) Public Library
Oak Lawn (Ill.) Public Library
Oakland (Calif.) Public Library
Ocean County (N.J.) Public Library
Oceanside (Calif.) Public Library
OCLC Inc.
Omaha (Neb.) Public Library
Onslow County (N.C.) Library
Oshkosh (Wis.) Public Library
Osterhout Free Library (Pa.)
Palm Springs (Calif.) Public Library
Palo Alto (Calif.) City Library
Pikes Peak Library District (Colo.)
Peoria (Ill.) Public Library
Free Library of Philadelphia (Pa.)
Phoenix (Ariz.) Public Library
Pioneer Multi-County System (Okla.)
Carnegie Library of Pittsburgh (Pa.)
Portsmouth (Va.) Public Library

Prince George's County (Md.) Memorial Library
Prince William County (Va.) Library
Providence (R.I.) Public Library
Queens Borough (N.Y.) Public Library
Redwood City (Calif.) Public Library
Richland County (S.C.) Public Library
Roanoke City (Va.) Public Library System
Rochester (Minn.) Public Library
Rochester Hills (Mich.) Public Library
Rosenberg Library (Tex.)
Roseville (Mich.) Public Library
Salt Lake City (Utah) Public Library
San Bernardino County (Calif.) Library
San Diego County (Calif.) Library
Santa Clara County (Calif.) Library
Santa Fe Regional Library (Fla.)
Scranton (Pa.) Public Library
Sioux Falls (S.D.) Public Library
Skokie (Ill.) Public Library
David R. Smith (consultant)
Southeastern Libraries Cooperative (Minn.)
Southern Maryland Regional Library
Spartanburg County (S.C.) Library
Spokane (Wash.) Public Library
Springfield (Mass.) City Library
St. Charles Public Library District (La.)
St. Cloud Great River Regional Library (Minn.)
Stoughton (Mass.) Public Library
Suffolk County (N.Y.) Cooperative Library System
Sunnyvale (Calif.) Public Library
Taunton (Mass.) Public Library
Tucson (Ariz.) Public Library
Tulsa City-County (Okla.) Library
Turner Subscriptions
Twin Falls (Idaho) Public Library
Ventura County Library Service Agency (Calif.)
Vigo County (Ind.) Public Library
Virginia Beach (Va.) Public Library
Volusia County (Fla.) Public Library; Deltonia, Holly Hill, Ormond Beach, and S. Cornelia Young Memorial branches
Watertown (Mass.) Free Public Library
Waukegan (Ill.) Public Library
Way Public Library (Ohio)
Weber County (Utah) Public Library
Webster Parish (La.) Library
West Bloomfield Township (Mich.) Public Library
West Hartford (Conn.) Public Library
Western Massachusetts Regional Library System

Westerville (Ohio) Public Library
Wicomico County (Md.) Free Library
Willows (Calif.) Public Library

Wissahickon Valley (Pa.) Public Library
Worthington (Ohio) Public Library

About This Book

PLANNING AND ROLE SETTING FOR PUBLIC LIBRARIES: A MANUAL OF OPTIONS AND PROCEDURES presents a planning process for public libraries. It also introduces a set of public library "roles" for librarians to use in choosing the most appropriate roles their library should fulfill in the community. The manual guides users through a process of reviewing existing conditions and services, defining the library's roles and mission, setting goals and objectives, choosing strategies to achieve the objectives, and evaluating the results of the process.

This planning manual is not a revision of *A Planning Process for Public Libraries*. Rather, the manual is a new approach to public library planning. The manual offers a new and simplified process intended to take into consideration these suggestions:

- Offer specific direction for how library planners should prepare to engage in the planning process
- Limit the amount of needs assessment and data collection material in the planning process
- Describe a *range* of levels of effort that a library might commit to planning
- Describe a set of typical service roles from which the most appropriate roles for a particular library can be identified
- Specify possible outlines for a public library planning document
- Detail procedures for implementing the library's plan.

Perhaps most importantly, librarians asked for a planning process that is easy to use, flexible, and doable. This planning manual has been developed with these suggestions in mind.

Audience

This manual is intended primarily for small (libraries with at least one full-time professional librarian) and medium-sized libraries, regional systems, and for state library agencies to use for public library development. Very small libraries (less than one full-time professional staff member) may find some useful ideas to adapt to their circumstances. Such libraries are especially encouraged to work with their state library agencies to make the best use of this manual. Very large or experienced libraries may require more detailed planning techniques than those offered in this manual. Nonetheless, this manual may serve as a beginning from which the planning effort can expand.

Purpose

The purpose of the manual is to provide public librarians with a tool to improve library management, increase overall library effectiveness, and assess the quality of library services. It is based on the assumption that planning provides a powerful means to better allocate existing resources, identify service priorities, demonstrate accountability, and accomplish stated objectives—regardless of library size, local community conditions, and funding levels.

But planning, in and of itself, is not a panacea for increased library effectiveness. No planning manual can hope to be "all things to all people." Instead, this one offers a *general approach* for public library planning. Librarians should use those techniques most appropriate to their situation and adapt others.

The manual is intended to be a "self-help" tool. Most public librarians should be able to use this manual without additional outside assistance. Successful use of the manual does not require sophisticated statistical skills. The skills most essential are a commitment to providing high-quality services, a desire to improve the overall managerial effectiveness of the library, good judgment, common sense, and a vision of excellence.

Throughout the manual, options are offered for varying levels of effort that can be committed to the planning process. When using the manual, librarians should carefully consider the level of effort that they can realistically commit to the overall planning process and to individual planning steps.

A number of workforms are included in the manual. To illustrate the discussion in the text, a reduced version of each workform is included as a figure at the point in the text where the workform is first introduced. A set of full-size workforms is also included as Appendix B. It is important to note that, depending on individual library situations, it is likely that these workforms may need to augmented, adapted, or otherwise changed before they can be used effectively in a specific library.

Increasing Library Excellence

There is no magic formula for library excellence—many factors contribute to the quality of a public library. But regardless of the specific situation of a particular library, some basic prerequisites are needed. First, librarians must be able to describe accurately the existing condition of the library and the factors affecting that condition. Second, they must have a vision and be able to state clearly what the condition and services of the library *should be.* And finally, they must be able to implement activities and evaluate their progress in reaching this vision.

Taken together, PLANNING AND ROLE SETTING FOR PUBLIC LIBRARIES: A MANUAL OF OPTIONS AND PROCEDURES and *Output Measures for Public Libraries: A Manual for Standardized Procedures,* second edition, provide a tool for librarians wishing to increase the excellence of their libraries. Use of these two manuals, on an ongoing basis, will provide a framework within which the library's vision of excellence can be nurtured and realized.

CHARLES R. MCCLURE NANCY A. VAN HOUSE
AMY OWEN DOUGLAS L. ZWEIZIG MARY JO LYNCH

January 1987

Introduction

Excellence in public library service is not an idle dream. In spite of the multifaceted character of the nation's public libraries and the diverse communities they serve, excellence is achieved daily. As you work toward excellence in your library, three principles are worth noting:

• Excellence must be defined locally—it results when library services match community needs, interests, and priorities.
• Excellence is possible for both small and large libraries—it rests more on commitment than on unlimited resources.
• Excellence is a moving target—even when achieved, excellence must continually be maintained.

To achieve excellence is to realize a vision. The planning process presented in this manual can help you articulate that vision and take the concrete actions necessary to bring it into reality for your library. Planning is dynamic: it provides choices and options, enabling you to shape the future of your library by making informed decisions about services, staff, and financial resources. This manual presents a flexible planning process, one that gives you options for:

• Preparing for planning tasks
• Gathering information about your library and the community it serves
• Selecting roles and defining a mission
• Establishing goals and objectives
• Selecting activities and tasks to attain goals and objectives
• Reporting the results of planning activities
• Evaluating accomplishments and recommending future actions.

The purpose of this manual is to help public librarians plan more successfully. It can be used by a wide range of libraries—those with a single full-time professional librarian and those with many professional staff. Librarians planning less formally as well as those with a requirement for greater formality and structure can adapt this process to meet their needs.

Because planning and measurement are closely linked, this manual frequently refers to its companion volume, *Output Measures for Public Libraries,* second edition (Nancy A. Van House, Mary Jo Lynch, Charles R. McClure, Douglas Zweizig, and Eleanor Jo Rodger; Chicago: American Library Association, 1987), hereafter referred to as *OMPL,* second edition. Using these two manuals together provides a solid foundation for library planning and measurement—your tools for achieving excellence.

The Planning Cycle

The planning cycle is the time each library takes to move through the major phases of planning and implementation. The length of this time varies from library to library. For most, a complete planning cycle lasts three to five years. Once established, the library's role choices, mission statement, and goals generally remain unchanged throughout the planning cycle.

Within the planning cycle are several objectives cycles. These shorter cycles include monitoring the library's activities, revising or developing new objectives and activities as needed, and continuing implementation. In addition, the first objectives cycle includes an evaluation of the planning process—the budget, staff time, participant roles, planning schedule, and other factors. Each objectives cycle thus forms a minicycle within the overall planning cycle. The objectives cycle can be tied to the library's annual budgeting process, although some libraries may take longer than one year to complete an objectives cycle—especially the first cycle.

The Reviewing Results phase of planning concludes the planning cycle and prepares the library to begin its next full cycle. This phase evaluates the results of planning and reviews the effectiveness of the planning process over the full cycle. The reviewers then transmit recommendations from the cycle just completed to the next. Figure 1 shows the relationships among the components of the basic planning cycle.

Phases in the Planning Process

The planning process has seven major phases: Planning to Plan, Looking Around, Developing Roles and Mission, Writing Goals and Objectives, Taking Action, Writing the Planning Document, and Reviewing Results. Each phase and its associated steps are covered in a separate chapter.

This manual presents the planning phases in a recommended order. Some libraries, however, may vary this approach. For example, some libraries may select roles and define a mission statement before Looking Around. Such an approach is workable if planners review the roles selected in light of the results of Looking Around. Or, a library might assess its current services with output measures and use the results as a stimulus for formal planning. No matter how you begin the planning process, this manual assumes that the full planning process will eventually be completed.

Planning to Plan

Prior to launching the planning process, each library organizes for the work ahead. Library planners make decisions that shape the planning process to the library's needs and resources, and coordinate planning with other management activities. They also define the responsibilities of major planning participants and organize and train the planning committee.

Looking Around

Looking Around collects information about the library and the community it serves. This information helps library planners plan more effectively. Planners identify the information needed for planning, gather that information, and study its importance for later planning decisions.

Developing Roles and Mission

This chapter describes eight distinct roles, or service profiles, which public libraries may emphasize in providing services to their communities. Library planners determine which roles are to receive a major commitment in their library and which are to be supported only minimally. The library's mission statement is a concise expression of the roles chosen for emphasis. It guides decisions in later planning phases and acts as a job description, helping the library to communicate its service focus to the public, elected officials, and staff.

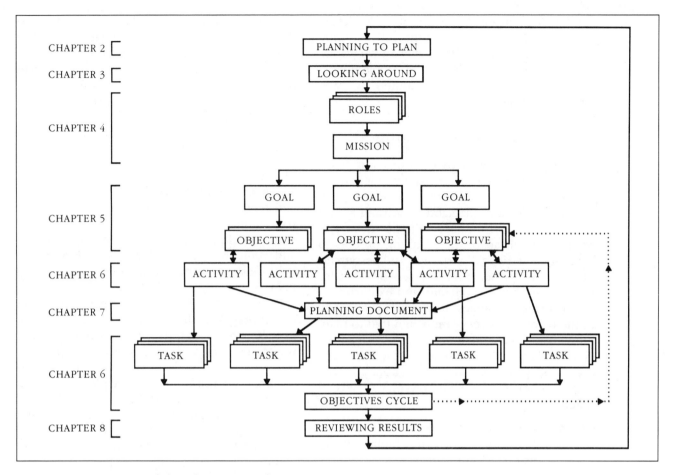

FIGURE 1   Overview of the Planning Cycle

Writing Goals and Objectives

Goals and objectives translate the library's role choices and mission into statements of desired ends or targets. Goals are long-range and represent a vision of excellence in library service. Objectives are specific, time limited, and measurable or verifiable. Taken together, goals and objectives provide a framework for implementation and evaluation.

Taking Action

Taking Action produces tangible evidence of the library's planning. Library planners identify possible activities to implement the goals and objectives and select the activities best suited to the library's circumstances and resources. As these activities are implemented, the planning perspective shifts. The staff implement, monitor, and evaluate the activities, and the planning committee reviews the planning process and prepares the planning document. This leads the library into the objectives cycle. The objectives

cycle is repeated, usually annually, until the library senses a need for change in its overall mission and the goals established at the beginning of the planning cycle.

Writing the Planning Document

The library's formal report of its planning activities is an excellent opportunity for communication with the public and with the library staff. This chapter presents options for the format and content of the planning document which each library can adapt for its own purposes.

Reviewing Results

After three to five years, the library is ready to begin a new planning cycle. In this planning phase, library planners first review the plan—the activities implemented and the extent to which they have accomplished the objectives, goals, roles, and mission statement. Next, planners review the evaluation of the planning process completed at the end of the first objectives cycle and assess the process over the full planning cycle. Finally, the results of these reviews are summarized, producing a set of recommendations for the next planning committee to use in a new planning cycle.

Levels of Effort in Planning

Planning is a human activity. It deals in possibilities, contingencies and change, not certainties, absolutes, and permanence. Effective planning is flexible and adaptable. Choosing a level of effort is one of the most significant ways in which you can adapt the planning process to your library's needs, purposes, and resources. This manual presents three levels of effort for each phase—basic, moderate, and extensive.

This manual assumes that librarians engaged in the planning process are committed to planning regardless of the library's size. Basic, moderate, and extensive levels of effort will all yield acceptable planning results. Each library's level-of-effort choice reflects the interplay of several different factors.

- *Participants:* the more individuals and the more groups represented, the higher the library's level of effort for planning.
- *Resources:* higher levels of effort call for a proportionally greater commitment of the library staff's time and larger expenditures from the library's budget.
- *Library context:* libraries serving a community with rapid growth or change, a complex and diverse population, shifting economic conditions, or libraries facing a major change in funding may need to plan at a higher level of effort.
- *Planning purposes:* what the library expects the planning process to accomplish may affect the level of effort chosen for some planning phases.
- *Planning structure:* libraries planning at a basic level of effort may approach many planning activities informally; but as library complexity increases, the planning structure becomes more formal, thus increasing the level of effort.
- *Planning schedule:* some libraries may complete their first objectives cycle over a very short time period; higher levels of effort may require twelve to eighteen months to complete.

In making level-of-effort choices, you need not set the same level of effort for all planning phases. The level of effort determined for the planning process as a whole sets a framework. But planners may commit varying levels of effort to major phases within the process and to specific steps within each planning phase. "Level of Effort Boxes" in the chapters ahead offer guidance for basic, moderate, and extensive levels of effort.

A Planning Road Map

There are many routes to successful planning. This manual is like a road map. It indicates routes and terrain, but you select the best route for your library after determining where you are now, your library's resources, its planning needs, and your chosen planning destination. These decisions are central to Chapter 2, Planning to Plan.

For now, begin to think about how much time your library can devote to planning, what you expect it to accomplish, and what you might want to emphasize during the planning process. For example, if your library has never conducted a formal needs assessment, Chapter 3, Looking Around, may be very useful. If your library is experienced in planning, you may take less time with Chapter 2, Planning to Plan.

Figure 2 reflects one likely route for a library completing the planning cycle for the first time. It lays out the major tasks ahead and is based on the steps presented in each chapter of this manual. The route for subsequent objectives cycles will vary from this pattern, as may the route you develop for your library.

Benefits of Planning

No planner can control or foresee the future. Even the best crystal ball is cloudy. Yet librarians must make choices, and planning provides a foundation for making choices. Sound planning leads to excellence in library service by:

- Helping librarians identify options and possibilities
- Encouraging librarians to consider the needs of the library's clientele and the community at large and to monitor trends in the environment
- Giving direction to library services through the roles chosen for emphasis and the library's mission
- Encouraging creative thinking about library programs, services, and activities
- Focusing attention on efficiency (How well is the library doing?) and effectiveness (Is the library doing the right things?)

CHAPTER 2: PLANNING TO PLAN
Step 1: Clarify Planning Purposes
Step 2: Balance the Library's Level of Effort for Planning
Step 3: Define Responsibilities for Planning
Step 4: Allocate Resources to Planning Activities
Step 5: Establish a Planning Schedule
Step 6: Establish the Planning Committee
Step 7: Educate Planning Participants

START

CHAPTER 3: LOOKING AROUND
Step 1: Determine Level of Effort
Step 2: Prepare for Looking Around
Step 3: Decide What Information Is Needed
Step 4: Gather the Information
Step 5: Study the Information
Step 6: Report the Results

CHAPTER 4: DEVELOPING ROLES AND MISSION
Step 1: Determine Level of Effort
Step 2: Study Library Roles
Step 3: Select Library Roles
Step 4: Prioritize Library Roles
Step 5: Write the Mission Statement

CHAPTER 5: WRITING GOALS AND OBJECTIVES
Step 1: Determine Level of Effort
Step 2: Review Existing Information
Step 3: Generate and Screen Goals
Step 4: Generate and Screen Objectives
Step 5: Make Objectives Measurable
Step 6: Write Draft Set of Goals and Objectives
Step 7: Rank Objectives
Step 8: Review the Final Goals and Objectives Statement

CHAPTER 6: TAKING ACTION
Step 1: Determine Level of Effort
Step 2: Identify Possible Activities to Accomplish Each Objective
Step 3: Select Activities
Step 4: Change the Planning Perspective

CHAPTER 6: TAKING ACTION
Step 5: Manage Implementation
Step 6: Monitor the Implementation Process
Step 7: Review Objectives and Activities

CHAPTER 7: WRITING THE PLANNING DOCUMENT
Step 1: Prepare to Write the Planning Document
Step 2: Determine Level of Effort
Step 3: Write the Planning Document
Step 4: Review the Planning Document
Step 5: Obtain Formal Approval
Step 6: Present/Promote the Planning Document

CHAPTER 8: REVIEWING RESULTS
Step 1: Determine Level of Effort
Step 2: Review the Plan
Step 3: Review the Planning Process
Step 4: Recycle the Information

CONTINUE

FIGURE 2   Sample Planning Road Map

- Helping librarians set priorities for allocating resources
- Providing feedback, allowing library staff to learn, adapt, and improve the library's performance
- Encouraging organizational, program, and individual accountability
- Orienting librarians toward the future.

The planning process is essential for managing library service effectively. It helps the library achieve the best possible fit between its service programs and the needs and expectations of its community. Successful planning leads to successful libraries and to excellence in library services.

The next chapter, Planning to Plan, describes how the planning process can be tailored to your library's circumstances. As you shape the process to meet your library's needs and resources, the planning process described in this manual will cease to be "*The* Planning Process" and will become "*Our* Planning Process." This redefinition will breathe life into the planning process, moving its recommendations into reality.

Planning to Plan

2

Preparation, the focus of this planning phase, is central to successful planning. The steps in this chapter help you choose options for tailoring the planning process to your library's needs, purposes, and resources. These steps are:

1. Clarify planning purposes
2. Balance the library's level of effort for planning
3. Define responsibilities for planning
4. Allocate resources to planning activities
5. Establish a planning schedule
6. Establish the planning committee
7. Educate planning participants.

Planning to Plan lays the foundation for all planning activities. The decisions made during this step are interrelated and affect later planning phases. For example, the planning budget should anticipate any costs associated with gathering information (Chapter 3) or publishing a planning report (Chapter 7). Before beginning this phase, therefore, those involved in Planning to Plan should become familiar with the overall planning process. A general reading of this manual is recommended.

In addition, libraries with prior experience in planning may wish to evaluate recommendations from earlier planning activities. What worked? What could have been done differently? Libraries that have completed a full planning cycle using this process can incorporate during Planning to Plan any recommendations produced during the Reviewing Results phase (Chapter 8) of the previous cycle.

Preliminary Considerations

Level of Effort for Planning to Plan

Because Planning to Plan prepares the library for the rest of the planning process, its decisions

Level of Effort for
Planning to Plan

Basic

Library planners discuss Planning to Plan steps informally. Decisions are largely based on the planners' working knowledge of the library's planning needs and financial resources. The results of Planning to Plan are summarized in a few paragraphs citing: two or three basic planning expectations with associated products; an overall level of effort for the planning process; names of planning committee members; the total dollar figure allotted to planning activities; and a target date for completing the first objectives cycle.

Moderate

Library planners discuss Planning to Plan steps on a more formal basis. Decisions are based on a review of the library's budget and a discussion of the library's planning needs. The results of Planning to Plan, reported in 2 to 3 pages, provide some detail to support the decisions made. The report may include: the library's planning expectations with a rationale for the planning products to be emphasized; an overall level of effort for the planning process balancing the levels of effort selected for major planning phases to the library's resources; brief statement of responsibility for individuals involved in the planning process; a budget statement similar to Workform A (see Figure 3) showing appropriate budget subcategories; and a planning chart similar to Figure 4 showing target dates for completing each planning phase.

Extensive

Decisions in Planning to Plan are based on a thorough review of the library's budget, planning needs, and factors in the library's environment that may affect planning activities. Special attention is given to coordinating the timing of planning recommendations with the library's budget cycle. The results of Planning to Plan, reported in 4 to 10 pages, record the decisions made and provide working tools for planners to use in the phases ahead. In addition to the material included at the Moderate Level of Effort, the report relates the levels of effort targeted for each planning phase to an expanded planning budget and schedule, and provides a more detailed discussion of staff responsibilities and reporting patterns.

are usually made by a small number of people prior to the formation of the library's planning committee. Depending on library circumstances and projected level of effort for this planning phase, these individuals may include:
• The director
• The director and chair of the library board
• The director and full board
• The director and one or two key staff members
• The director, chair of the library board, and one or two key staff members.
Generally, the higher the level of effort, the

larger the number of individuals involved and the more resources required. In addition, increased formality in decision making and more detailed record keeping are also characteristic of increased effort in this planning phase.

Keeping a Record
Record the decisions made during Planning to Plan, and keep this record until the conclusion of the complete planning cycle. This record is invaluable evidence of the library's original planning intentions. It will help you to:

- Document decisions made
- Communicate planning parameters consistently to the planning committee, other participants, and the community
- Complete the formal planning document (see Chapter 7, Writing the Planning Document)
- Lay a foundation for evaluating the overall planning cycle (see Chapter 8, Reviewing Results).

Planning and Public Relations

The planning process presents an unparalleled opportunity for effective public relations. It offers natural occasions to seek public input, to demonstrate the library's interest in serving the community effectively, and to promote library services. Plan now to take advantage of opportunities provided by each planning phase. Options for public relations include:

- News releases or special press coverage highlighting the results of major planning activities
- Articles placed in the library's newsletter or those sponsored by local government, employees' union, the state library, or the state professional association
- Reports at meetings of groups close to the library such as friends, staff associations, interested clubs or societies, and chamber of commerce groups
- Public hearings to receive comment and reactions to the plan during its development or to inform the public after its completion.

Public Libraries with Multiple Outlets

Several options for adapting the planning process are open to public libraries with multiple service outlets. These libraries must coordinate branch planning with planning done for the library as a whole. If the library's service area is similar from branch to branch, library-wide planning may be satisfactory. But branch level planning may be needed if branch service areas or clientele are different. Options include:

- Library-wide planning
- Combined library and branch planning
- Branch planning only.

The pattern the library expects to follow in other planning phases influences these choices. Chapter 4, Developing Roles and Mission, and Chapter 5, Writing Goals and Objectives, also discuss coordinating planning activities among the library and its branches.

Step 1: Clarify Planning Purposes

What do you expect the planning process to do for the library? What products will the planning process produce? Answering these questions enables you to focus planning efforts on the library's most immediate and pressing needs and to make better planning decisions. These answers also help communicate planning purposes to the planning committee, staff, elected officials, and the community. Libraries become involved in formal planning for many reasons. Some of the most common reasons include:

- Clarifying the value of the library to local government or the community
- Evaluating specific library services and activities
- Helping the library better allocate existing resources
- Helping the library prepare for changing circumstances in its funding or in the community
- Improving library management
- Establishing service priorities
- Fostering better communications within the library or between the library and the community
- Securing additional revenue for the library
- Improving the extent to which library services meet community needs and expectations
- Documenting the need for a new or expanded facility.

Take time now to determine which of these, or other, purposes best describe your situation. Relate your expectations to the specific planning products associated with each planning phase. For example, if you hope to improve the extent to which the library meets community needs, the report of Looking Around, Chapter 3, will deserve special attention. If you want to define a library mission, roles will be of critical importance. Relating expectations for the planning process to the products suggested in this manual also helps you determine how your library will balance its level-of-effort choices.

Step 2: Balance the Library's Level of Effort for Planning

How much effort will the library devote to planning? Even though commitment to planning may be high, practical matters, such as budget and staff availability, influence the answer to this question. While the overall level of effort (basic, moderate, or extensive) may appear obvious given the library's circumstances, the level of effort for each phase can vary. Now is the time to balance the level of effort set for each planning phase with the overall effort.

For example, one library's purpose is to articulate its value to the community through defining a mission, selecting roles, and establishing service priorities. If this library's circumstances dictate an overall moderate level of effort, library planners may counterbalance a high level of effort for Chapter 4, Developing Roles and Mission, and Chapter 6, Taking Action, with a basic level of effort for two or three other planning steps. Balancing the library's level of effort simplifies the allocation of library resources in Step 4 of this chapter.

Step 3: Define Responsibilities for Planning

Many groups work together during the planning process. Preparing a brief statement of each group's responsibilities fosters open communication and better understanding among planning participants. The following discussion covers typical responsibilities for major participant groups.

The Library Director

Leadership is the heart of the planning process. Responsibility for effective planning rests first with the library director who must have time, energy, and a *visible* commitment to managing the planning process. The director:

- Inspires planning participants
- Demonstrates commitment to effective planning and quality library services
- Creates a positive climate to support planning activities
- Obtains and allocates adequate resources to support the planning process
- Often chairs the planning committee.

The Planning Committee

Virtually all libraries form a planning committee. Seldom is successful organizational planning the work of one individual. Some libraries seek citizen representation on the planning committee; others do not. Planning committees may include any combination of the following: the director, key staff, board members, and citizens.

The larger the planning committee and the more groups represented, the higher the library's level of effort for planning. Generally, 7 to 9 individuals is a workable number. If citizens are not represented on the planning committee, the library can still seek citizen input by having individuals serve as informal reactors or advisers or by holding hearings.

The planning committee may assume a variety of responsibilities such as representing constituents, reviewing planning documents, completing specific tasks, recommending policies, etc. No committee is likely to undertake all these roles, and each library defines the committee's role differently. Determine what responsibilities your planning committee will undertake and how the planning committee relates to your board of trustees.

The Library Board

Most libraries operate under a board of trustees. The director and the board, whether advisory or governing, share a vested interest in the results of the library's planning. Therefore, involvement of library board members in the planning process is important. Often, one or more board members serve on the planning committee. In small libraries, the board itself may constitute the planning committee.

The Library Staff

Involvement of library staff—especially heads of major service units or branches—is vital for successful library planning. Staff are "doers" in the planning process. They support the planning committee, carry out various planning activities, and react to drafts of planning documents. Ultimately, staff implement planning recommendations. In some libraries, staff serve on the planning committee.

Consultants

Some libraries find the services of a consultant helpful during the planning process. A consultant may act as a neutral sounding board, serve as a lightning rod for controversial issues, facilitate group discussions, or provide technical expertise and experience with planning techniques. Not every library will use a consultant, and some libraries will use a variety of consultants for different tasks. Possible sources of consulting assistance include interested community members or staff from the state library, a regional library system, library school, or local government agency.

Step 4: Allocate Resources to Planning Activities

Planning need not be costly. Effective planning is done in many libraries without a large direct financial outlay. Often staff time is the major cost of a planning effort. This suggests that allocating resources to planning activities has two parts: budgeting for direct financial costs and managing staff time. Demands on library resources during planning are affected by many of the decisions just considered—planning purposes and products, participant roles, and level of effort. Budgeting and managing staff time helps you make sure that the planning activities projected are reasonable, given the library's circumstances.

In preparing a planning budget, most libraries project only direct costs, such as planning committee expenses, training, and data collection. Adapt Workform A, Simple Planning Budget (see Figure 3), to your library's circumstances to establish a basic planning budget.

Projecting staff involvement in the planning process is an important part of Planning to Plan. For many libraries, planning is a new activity, and without the luxury of added staff, planning must be fitted into current staff assignments. Estimating staff time for planning helps determine when extra help (volunteers or temporary staff) may be needed or when staff must be released from current job assignments to take on plan-

ning duties. Staff members need to clearly understand what is expected of them.

Some directors translate projections of staff time into cost figures. They do so because:

• These costs are real and affect the library's ongoing service programs
• Knowing these costs helps the library evaluate the cost-effectiveness of the planning process.

If you wish to determine the cost of staff time, list the staff members to be involved in the planning process, estimate how many hours each will spend per week or per month on planning tasks, and multiply that estimate by the staff member's actual salary plus benefits. As planning begins, each staff member should regularly report the time actually spent on planning so that the estimate can be compared to the actual staff cost.

Step 5: Establish a Planning Schedule

Developing a planning schedule keeps the process moving ahead. A planning chart (see Figure 4) helps participants better understand how their responsibilities tie into other planning activities. Time periods across the chart can be varied as needed (day, week, or month), as can the detail of the tasks listed down the left side of the form. As an alternative to developing planning charts, libraries with microcomputers

WORKFORM A   Simple Planning Budget

Budget Category	Projected Expenditure
Planning Committee: (Consider number of meetings, travel and food costs)	_____
Consultants: (Consider desired scope of consultant activities)	_____
Data Collection: (Consider level of effort for Looking Around)	_____
General Costs:	
Copying	_____
Printing	_____
Extra telephone charges	_____
Extra postage charges	_____
Additional staff support	_____
Total:	_____

FIGURE 3   Reduced Workform A: Simple Planning Budget

WORKFORM B   Planning Chart

Task	Person	Month											
		1	2	3	4	5	6	7	8	9	10	11	12
1.													
2.													
3.													
4.													
5.													
6.													
7.													
8.													
9.													
10.													
11.													
12.													
Notes and Explanations:													

FIGURE 4   Reduced Workform B: Planning Chart

may wish to investigate the possibility of using project management software. Such software packages provide a flexible way to document staff assignments, schedule tasks, and display graphically task interrelationships.

Some planning recommendations have financial implications. For this reason, coordinating the planning process with the library's budgeting cycle has advantages. The most important coordination point is the Taking Action phase, Chapter 6. Any recommendations with budgetary impact need to be ready in time to be included in the library's budget request for the following year.

Figure 5 shows a sample chart for a library which has scheduled its planning process to culminate in April and May so that the budget submitted to local government the following June reflects planning recommendations. The time periods shown in Figure 5 will vary from library to library because each library takes a different length of time to move through the planning phases.

Step 6: Establish the Planning Committee

In libraries using a planning committee composed of staff and board members, the director usually appoints the planning committee. For libraries using citizens on the planning committee, the process is more involved. Begin by identifying a wide pool of names for potential committee members. The director, board, key staff, members of the Friends of the Library group, and local government representatives may participate in this activity. Individuals nominated should have a genuine interest in the library, the ability to make a meaningful contribution, and time to commit to the planning process. The list of potential committee members may need approval from an authority beyond the library director, such as the library board or local government.

Once the names are approved, the director or president of the library board invites nominees to serve on the planning committee. This invi-

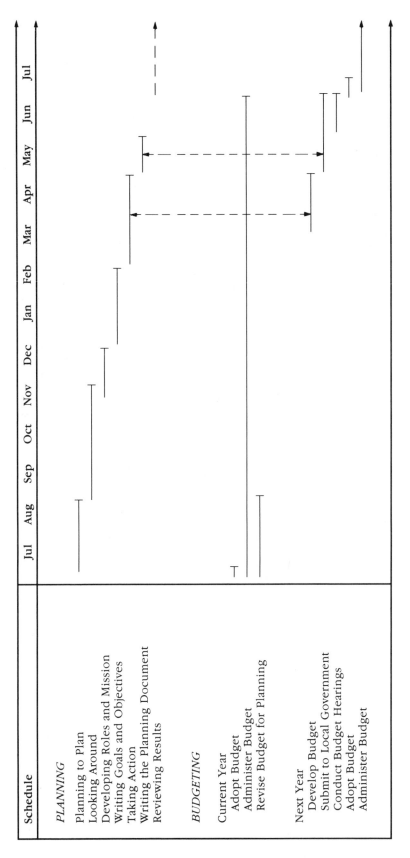

FIGURE 5   Relating Planning and Budgeting for the Morningside Public Library

tation is usually extended in the form of a letter. Because accepting this invitation entails a commitment, the letter of invitation should clearly indicate:

• The purpose of the planning process
• The planning committee's role and responsibilities
• The date, time, and place of the first planning committee meeting
• How often and, if possible, at what times the group will meet
• The timetable set for the planning process
• Limits of the planning committee's authority and its relationship to the library board and local government
• Whether any expenses incurred (for example, mileage and telephone calls) are reimbursable.

Step 7: Educate Planning Participants

Those involved in Planning to Plan already have a basic understanding of the planning process. But as the process begins, others involved with or affected by the library's planning need to understand the planning process, its purposes, and activities. In addition, citizen members of the planning committee need information about the library's services and policies, current financial status, and history in the community. Some of this education occurs as the planning process develops. Other options include:

• Providing a basic set of written materials (for example, annual reports, past plans, a written charge) for the planning committee
• Conducting brief orientation sessions at the start of each committee meeting
• Scheduling workshops for orientation and training

• Providing tours of the library's facilities or the community
• Having a consultant build a team spirit and introduce basic planning concepts.

The library has now completed its Planning to Plan decisions. It has set the scope and schedule of its planning activities, allocated its resources, and has organized and prepared the planning committee. The library and planning committee are now ready to begin the next planning phase, Looking Around.

Sources for Additional Information

Fersko-Weiss, Henry. "Streamline Your Simple Projects." *Personal Computing* 10 (November 1986): 89–91, 93, 95.

This article describes the uses and advantages of project management software packages designed for microcomputers, reviews several different packages, and provides tips for choosing a package appropriate to your needs.

Jackson, Inez L. and E. Ramsey. *Library Planning and Budgeting.* New York: Franklin Watts, 1986.

This publication has useful information on establishing cost centers and on relating the library's planning and budgeting cycles.

Rosenberg, Philip. *Cost Finding for Public Libraries, A Manager's Handbook.* Chicago: American Library Association, 1985.

For libraries wishing to establish a formal planning budget, this publication provides a common-sense approach for defining direct and indirect costs and for calculating costs for various library activities.

Samuels, Alan R. "Organizational Climate and Library Change." In *Strategies for Library Administration,* ed. Charles R. McClure and Alan Samuels, pp. 421–431. Littleton, Colo.: Libraries Unlimited, 1982.

This chapter describes an approach to assessing a library's organizational climate prior to initiating a major activity, such as a planning process, intended to produce change in the organization.

Looking Around

Looking Around, the process of collecting information about the library and its community, is one of the most interesting phases in the planning process. It is a process of discovery, of finding answers to such basic questions as: What kind of community does the library serve? Who lives there? What do residents expect from the library? Information about the community and its residents helps you understand what services may be needed. Information about the library helps you understand how well the library is doing its job. Taken collectively, this information assists the planning process by:

- Identifying factors in the library's environment that may affect the provision of services
- Revealing community needs for library services
- Demonstrating to community decision makers the library's understanding of its services and its community
- Suggesting possible library roles, goals, and objectives.

This phase in the planning process is closely linked with the next, Developing Roles and Mission (Chapter 4). In fact, you may reverse the order of these two phases. Placing the Looking Around phase first helps the planning committee consider library and community conditions as they select roles. Developing Roles and Mission first can help the planning committee focus its Looking Around activities. Either approach is workable.

Looking Around has six basic steps:

1. Determine level of effort
2. Prepare for Looking Around
3. Decide what information is needed
4. Gather the information

5. Study the information
6. Report the results.

Step 1: Determine Level of Effort

Level of effort for Looking Around is directly proportional to the amount of information the planning committee decides to gather and the sources used to obtain that information. Therefore, the planning committee's "information appetite" must be tailored to match the library's staff time and financial resources. Three factors are important.

- The time available for this planning phase: some information is readily available; other information may take longer to assemble.
- The diversity present in the library's community: a relatively homogeneous community can be described more easily than a complex community.
- The rate of change in the library's community: rapid change may indicate a need for more comprehensive information.

At basic and moderate levels of effort, the planning committee selects only a small set of data (see Step 3) and confines its information gathering to existing sources of information (see Step 4). At an extensive level of effort, the planning committee conducts a much more thorough analysis of the library's environment and may use data collection methods beyond the scope of this manual, such as surveying. The citations at the end of this chapter can provide guidance for these methods.

Step 2: Prepare for Looking Around

The planning committee and library staff both have an important role during Looking Around. Generally, the staff is responsible for gathering and assembling the information required by the planning committee. The committee determines what information it needs and studies the information collected. This step prepares the planning committee and staff for these activities.

Assign Staff Responsibilities

The library director determines who will be responsible for gathering information during Looking Around. Usually one staff member is given the overall responsibility to gather, organize, and analyze the information requested by the planning committee. If possible, this person should have experience in reference or public services, be a good communicator, and a good organizer. Others on the library staff assist as needed. Ideally, staff assignments are made *before* the planning committee decides what information to collect. This allows those responsible, by working with the committee, to better understand what the committee needs and how the information might be used. If your library has a microcomputer, the use of word processing, database management, and spreadsheet software can make writing reports and analyzing and presenting information easier.

Prepare the Planning Committee

Two reviews can help the planning committee approach Looking Around more productively. First, review the basic guidelines for collecting information presented in Figure 6. These tips can help both librarians and planning committee members approach Looking Around in a positive, realistic framework.

Second, review with the committee the range of information that might be considered. In so doing, consider information about the library's community (Looking Around Outside) and information about the library itself (Looking Around Inside).

DO:	Consider both factual data and subjective impressions about the library, its services, and its community.
DO:	Take advantage of information already collected by others both within and outside the library.
DO:	Know in advance what use will be made of each piece of information collected.
DO:	Allow ample time to think about and interpret the information gathered.
DO:	Set a clear time schedule for Looking around activities.
DO:	Refer to *Output Measures for Public Libraries,* second edition, for measures and data collection methods suitable to the library.
	* * *
DON'T:	Allow Looking Around to become an end unto itself—all steps in the process are important.
DON'T:	Collect more information than the planning committee can use.
DON'T:	Conduct surveys unless the library can commit an extensive level of effort to Looking Around and has (or acquires) the necessary expertise.

FIGURE 6 General Do's and Don'ts for Looking Around

Level of Effort for
Looking Around

Basic

The library director assigns responsibility for collecting and organizing Looking Around information to a staff member. In very small libraries, the director may handle this task. The planning committee uses Workform C as a menu to select the information useful for its planning purposes. These items are gathered from existing information sources and organized by the staff. The planning committee discusses these findings and uses Workform D to identify the potential impact of the findings on library services and to determine possible library responses. This workform serves as the report of the Looking Around planning phase.

Moderate

The library director assigns responsibility for coordinating the collection and organization of Looking Around information to a staff member. Other library staff assist. The planning committee selects most items listed on Workform C and obtains trend and comparative information for many of the items. These items are gathered from existing information resources and organized by the staff. The planning committee discusses the findings and uses Workform D to identify the potential impact of the findings on library services and to determine possible library responses. The report of Looking Around activities and findings is brief, but follows the basic outline shown in Figure 10.

Extensive

The library director assigns responsibility for collecting and organizing Looking Around information to a staff committee. In addition to the items listed on Workform C, the planning committee develops an information needs list containing a broad range of additional information. Some of this information requires library staff to collect original data through measurement activities (such as those described in *OMPL*, second edition), surveying, interviewing, or other data collection methods. The staff use research skills and computer support to analyze the data, determine findings, and produce summary graphics. The planning committee discusses these findings at length, using Workform D to summarize the results of its discussion. The staff prepare a comprehensive report of Looking Around activities and findings based on the outline shown in Figure 10. In addition to its uses in the planning process, this report may be widely disseminated to the board, staff, local government, and the community.

LOOKING AROUND OUTSIDE

Communities and their residents differ. These differences translate into service demands on the library. For example, an actively growing community with a diverse, highly educated population will place different demands on the library than a community whose industries are declining and whose residents are predomi- nantly unemployed blue-collar workers. The categories below suggest types of information that the planning committee might obtain.

- *Demographics:* the age, sex, racial, ethnic, educational, and income levels of residents; family characteristics, such as single heads of household and family size; and community characteristics, such as the birth, death, and unemployment rates.

- *Economic conditions:* the mix of business, farming, manufacturing, and service sectors; tax base; and economic trends—growth, decline, and boom/bust cycles.
- *Social conditions:* educational and cultural institutions, clubs, societies, interest groups, religious groups, traditions, and community history.
- *Informational and educational services:* other nearby libraries; primary, secondary, and post-secondary educational institutions and nontraditional learning programs; newspapers and magazines; fee-based information services, bookstores, radio stations, and cable television.

LOOKING AROUND INSIDE

Looking Around Inside examines the library's current condition. All aspects of library services are fair game: building, collections, services, staff, management programs, and budget allocation. Libraries with multiple service outlets may study them individually or collectively and may evaluate communication and service patterns among the branches and central library. The categories listed below suggest types of information the planning committee might review. Many of the measures cited in the collection and services categories are discussed in *OMPL,* second edition. Libraries that lack information for these measures may gather that data now or in later objectives cycles.

- *Building:* age; condition; code compliance; patterns of traffic for workflow and patrons; signage; parking; appearance; location; handicapped access; visibility; space needs for the collection, patrons, and staff; and adequacy of mechanical systems.
- *Collection:* breadth and depth of library holdings; formats available; use patterns; age of the collection; condition of materials; the rate of additions or withdrawals; adequacy of the catalog (either online or manual); and measures of collection use such as fill rates and turnover rate.
- *Services:* number and type of services; number of patrons using services; effectiveness and extensiveness of services and programs (see *OMPL,* second edition); studies of particular service areas, such as the reference department; and interlibrary loan statistics and patterns.

- *Staff:* educational levels; salary and benefit comparisons with similar libraries; length of service time with the library; satisfaction with current library services or conditions; staff workloads; and opportunities for training or continuing education.
- *Management:* efficiency and effectiveness of internal operational units (cataloging, acquisitions, administration, etc.); management skills; administrative procedures; relationships with other libraries and networking activities.
- *Budget allocation:* adequacy of budget; comparisons with similar libraries; and analysis of resource allocations among budget categories (personnel, collections, and operations), among branches and the central library, or among services (Children's, Young Adult, or Adult Services; Technical Services; Outreach or Audiovisual Services, etc.).

Step 3: Decide What Information Is Needed

To decide what information is important for planning, the planning committee identifies a focus for its information-gathering activities and agrees on the final list of information to be gathered. This manual presents two tools for use in this step: a list of basic community and library characteristics (Figure 7) and an information needs list (Figure 8).

The amount of potential information about the library and its community is staggering. The planning committee needs to make sure it gets the *right* information—the information most important and most useful for decision making. Too much information may overwhelm the committee, and too little information or the wrong information can mislead the committee or limit its vision. Identifying a focus for collecting information helps the planning committee make its Looking Around activities as productive as possible. Libraries Looking Around at a basic or moderate level of effort can use Workform C, Options for Library Planning Information (see Figure 7), to focus their collection of information. The information needs list (Figure 8) is most useful at an extensive level of effort.

Using Workform C

Workform C presents a set of community and library characteristics useful for many libraries. Typically, the information shown is readily available from printed information sources,

WORKFORM C, Part A Options for Library Planning Information

COMMUNITY CHARACTERISTICS

Information on Individuals	Current/Local	Comparative
Percentage of population under 5 years of age	_____	_____
Percentage of population 5 to 17 years of age	_____	_____
Percentage of population 17 to 65 years of age	_____	_____
Percentage of population over 65 years of age	_____	_____
Per capita personal income	_____	_____
Percentage of persons below poverty level	_____	_____
Percentage of population over 25 with		
12 or more years of school completed	_____	_____
16 or more years of school completed	_____	_____

Other: (Cite other statistics, describe trends or characteristics)

_____ _____ _____
_____ _____ _____
_____ _____ _____

Information on Families and Households	Current/Local	Comparative
Total number of households	_____	_____
Average number of persons per household	_____	_____
Total number of families	_____	_____
Total number of nonfamily households	_____	_____
Total number of one-person households	_____	_____
Median family income	_____	_____
Percentage of families below poverty line	_____	_____

Racial/language/ethnic groups: (List appropriate groups and percentages for your community.)

_____
_____
_____

Other: (Cite other statistics, describe trends or characteristics)

_____ _____ _____
_____ _____ _____
_____ _____ _____

WORKFORM C, Part B Options for Library Planning Information (continued)

Information on the Community	Current/Local	Comparative
Total population of legal service area (See *OMPL*, second edition)	_____	_____
Assessed Valuation per Capita	_____	_____
Percentage of labor force in manufacturing	_____	_____
Percentage of labor force in wholesale and related services	_____	_____
Percentage of labor force in professional and related groups	_____	_____
Percentage of labor force in government	_____	_____
Percentage of labor force self-employed	_____	_____
Percentage of labor force in other locally significant industry (Specify:)		
	_____	_____
Unemployment rate	_____	_____
Number of religious groups or organizations	_____	_____
Number of schools	_____	_____
Elementary	_____	_____
Secondary	_____	_____
High School	_____	_____
Vocational/technical	_____	_____
Colleges/universities	_____	_____
Number of hospitals	_____	_____

Other libraries, information providers, museums, or recreational facilities (List or give the total number for each category)

_____
_____

	Current/Local	Comparative
Number of newspapers	_____	_____
Number of radio and television stations	_____	_____
Types and number of clubs and organizations		

_____
_____

Other: (Cite other statistics, describe trends or characteristics)

_____ _____ _____
_____ _____ _____
_____ _____ _____

WORKFORM C, Part C Options for Library Planning Information (continued)

LIBRARY CHARACTERISTICS

Collection	Current/Local	Comparative
Number of volumes	_____	_____
Formats available (List)		

Other: (Comment on collection scope, currency, subject strengths, etc.)

_____
_____

Staff:

	Current/Local	Comparative
Total number of employees	_____	_____
Total number of full-time equivalent employees	_____	_____
Number of professional employees	_____	_____
Number of paraprofessional employees	_____	_____
Number of clerical employees	_____	_____
Number of maintenance workers	_____	_____

Other: (Describe any other important staff characteristics)

Financial Resources:

	Current/Local	Comparative
Total operating budget	_____	_____
Expenditures per capita	_____	_____

Facilities:

	Current/Local	Comparative
Number of service outlets	_____	_____
Total hours of service per week at all service outlets	_____	_____
Total number of square feet at all service outlets	_____	_____
Total seating capacity at all service outlets	_____	_____
Number of meeting rooms at all service outlets	_____	_____
Equipment available for public use (list)		

Other: (Describe any other important features such as layout, parking, accessibility, etc.)

_____
_____

WORKFORM C, Part D Options for Library Planning Information (continued)

Output Measures (See *OMPL*, second edition)	Current/Local	Comparative
Browsers' Fill Rate	_____	_____
Circulation per Capita	_____	_____
Document Delivery	_____	_____
In-Library Materials Use per Capita	_____	_____
Library Visits per Capita	_____	_____
Program Attendance per Capita	_____	_____
Reference Completion Rate	_____	_____
Reference Transactions per Capita	_____	_____
Registrations as a Percentage of the Population	_____	_____
Subject and Author Fill Rate	_____	_____
Title Fill Rate	_____	_____
Turnover Rate	_____	_____

Other: (Specify any other relevant measures)

_____ _____ _____
_____ _____ _____
_____ _____ _____
_____ _____ _____
_____ _____ _____

FIGURE 7   Reduced Workform C: Options for Library Planning Information

agencies and organizations, and existing library statistics. Planners can review these characteristics, weigh their relative value for the library's planning, and select the most useful items.

Libraries planning for the first time or those Looking Around at a basic level of effort may use Workform C as a menu, selecting items of interest. Information not collected now can be gathered in later objectives cycles. Libraries Looking Around at a moderate level of effort collect most items on Workform C and make an extra effort to collect comparative information.

Comparative information helps place current data in perspective. The "Comparative" column on Workform C could contain as appropriate: historic information (such as library service statistics from last year or 5 years ago); projected community data (such as population projections for 5 or 10 years into the future); or comparisons with other libraries (peer libraries within the state or nationally). Use whatever comparative information is meaningful and useful for your library's planning purposes.

Using the Information Needs List

Libraries Looking Around at an extensive level of effort can use an information needs list to keep track of information of potential planning interest. Figure 8 shows part of such a list prepared by a library placing a high priority on circulation of popular materials and services to students. Each library's list varies, reflecting its unique needs.

To develop an information needs list, the planning committee brainstorms and lists ideas for information that seem likely to be useful in planning. If possible, suggestions for the potential use of information items can be added to the list during the discussion. Ideas for information items can come from the committee's review of Looking Around Outside and Looking Around Inside, Workform C, or a consideration of the following perspectives:

• Planning committee perceptions
• Library measures
• Library roles.

PLANNING COMMITTEE PERCEPTIONS

Just as librarians are aware of their library's current service profile, members of the planning committee each have a sense of the community's history, neighborhoods, and businesses. They understand its social and economic life,

changes that are occurring, and the community's values and priorities.

These perceptions can help generate ideas for needed information. In a community experiencing dramatic change (such as a town with boom/bust cycles), economic information may be vital for planning. A library in a community with a wide variety of educational and cultural resources may choose to look at its relationship with other providers of education and information in the community.

LIBRARY ROLES

During the next phase of the planning process (see Chapter 4), the library adopts roles. Most librarians already have a sense of the roles currently emphasized in their service programs. This sense can guide the gathering of information. For example, a library that places a high priority on services to elementary and secondary students is likely to be interested in the Formal Education Support Center role. This library might gather in-depth data about school enrollment trends, student patterns for using the library, school faculty awareness of library services, etc. Library planners may review the "Output Measures to Explore" and the "Critical Resources" described for each of the eight roles in Chapter 4 to help identify information useful for assessing the library's capacity to perform selected roles.

LIBRARY MEASURES

Measurement is the collection of data representing the state of the library, its services, and its users. Output measures provide objective data on the effectiveness of library services. Output measures are powerful tools for describing the library. They evaluate the services the library delivers and can help assess current levels of performance, identify problem areas, and monitor progress toward objectives.

Some libraries will choose to calculate basic performance measures derived from existing library statistics, such as circulation per capita, as part of Looking Around. Others may take time to complete more complex measures requiring surveying, such as fill rate measures. *OMPL,* second edition, contains procedures for these and other measures that can provide information useful during Looking Around. Appendix A lists these measures.

When a first draft of the information needs list is completed, the planning committee assesses its information appetite. How much effort will it take to collect the information? How does that

Information	Possible Source	Potential Use

Community population:
  % under 5 years of age
  % 5–17 years of age
  % over 65 years of age
	City and County Data Book
	  or State Planning Office
		Check projected student population
		Check current student population
		Has senior population grown in the
		  last 5 years?

Total Registered Borrowers	Library records	Get current + 5 years ago Any changes?

% of community aware of various
library services:
  Basic circulation services
  Children's story hours
  A/V services
  Kiosk displays in mall
  Reference services
  Interlibrary loan services
  Meeting rooms
	Survey	Is the library well known?
		Do we need to publicize some
		  services better?

Turnover rate: our library Turnover rate: other libraries	Library records State Library	How active is the collection? Comparisons with similar size libraries in state

Library Circulation
  Adult
  Juvenile
	Library records	Who accounts for what part of our
		  circulation?

% of students (K–12) who have
visited the library:
  within the last month
  within the last year
	Survey (Get data at the building
	  level)
		Which schools account for most of
		  our student use? How could we
		  target a library/faculty relations
		  program?

. . . and so forth		
Subject and Author Fill Rate	*OMPL,* 2nd ed./Survey	How well are we doing?.
Ratio of additions to total library holdings	Library records	Help in diagnosing the currency of the collection

NOTE: Prepared from the point of view of a library emphasizing circulation of popular materials and services to K–12 students.

FIGURE 8   Sample Information Needs List

effort compare to the original level of effort set for Looking Around? What are the benefits of the information listed in relation to the cost of gathering it? To answer these questions, it may be useful to group similar information items together. This can help the planning committee identify any redundancy or gaps in the list. If the first draft of the information needs list is too lengthy, the planning committee should trim the list.

Step 4: Gather the Information

Once the planning committee has decided what information it needs, the assigned library staff gather the information. This step includes organizing the information to be gathered, tapping existing information sources, and completing other information-gathering activities as needed.

Organize the Information to Be Gathered

First, review and organize the information items the planning committee has selected. A useful way to group the items is by the potential source or method of collecting the information. For example, one group consists of the information to be found in current library records. Another might include information about the community available in census data or at a local or state agency. A third grouping includes data that can only be obtained through completing procedures suggested in *OMPL,* second edition. For libraries Looking Around at an extensive level of effort, a fourth group might include surveying or other activities to collect original data.

Tap Existing Information Sources

A wide variety of existing information sources is available to library planners. Always use the most current, authoritative source available. High-quality information contributes to effective planning. Out-of-date population data, inaccurate financial information, or inconsistently compiled library service statistics are serious barriers to sound decision making.

PRINTED INFORMATION SOURCES

For city and county libraries, a variety of demographic information from the most recent census is readily available in the *City and County Data Book.* Other census publications, the statistical publications of state agencies, city or area directories, telephone books, atlases, almanacs, and newspapers are all possible sources.

GOVERNMENTAL AGENCIES AND OTHER ORGANIZATIONS

Local and state government offices are often good sources of information. Check with the state library, planning offices, economic development bureaus, tourism agencies, local boards of education, and tax or revenue departments. They may have updates to census information, demographic, economic, and business information, or information derived from community needs assessment or other planning studies. Nongovernmental agencies can provide information too. Chambers of commerce and trade associations assemble information on the community and the surrounding area.

In addition, planning documents developed by local government agencies, such as school districts or parks departments, often contain goals that affect library services. Statewide plans for library service developed by the state library agency or state professional association may also be useful.

LIBRARY STATISTICS AND LIBRARY LITERATURE

Current library statistics can provide a variety of information, and many library measures can be calculated using existing library records. Trends in these statistics and measures over the past few years can help the planning committee place in perspective and interpret current library performance. Check to see what statistical information about library services and trends is available on a regional, state, or national basis.

A review of library literature may reveal a variety of useful reports. National studies of libraries, library users, and adult readers may be of interest to the planning committee. Or, the staff may be able to locate articles providing information about a topic or service area of concern to the planning committee.

Complete Other Information-Gathering Activities as Needed

Many libraries, particularly those Looking Around at a basic level of effort, can find adequate information in existing information sources. Libraries devoting a greater level of effort to Looking Around often engage in original data collection. Options include:

- *Library walk-arounds and community drive-arounds:* Planners follow a route carefully planned to reveal the library or community in a comprehensive fashion. They look for answers to such questions as: What was surprising? Where was change evident? What types of people were encountered in the community, the library, or on the library staff?
- *Surveys:* Library surveys obtain information directly from individuals such as library users, students, and staff. Surveys may be done in-person, by telephone, mail, or by a variety of drop-off and pick-up methods. Surveys are flexible, adaptable, and efficient, but require careful design, pretesting, administration, and interpretation.
- *Interviews:* Interviews, like surveys, supplement statistical information by reflecting the views of individuals who might otherwise remain silent and by broadening citizen participation in library planning. Interviews may be targeted at groups or individuals. Effective interviewing requires care in selecting those interviewed, determining interview questions, and organizing and interpreting the results.
- *Structured observation:* Structured observation is a technique that studies specific activities, tasks, or events. Unlike surveying and interviewing, individuals performing the tasks are generally unaware that their activities are being analyzed. Like the techniques above, structured observation requires thorough preliminary planning and sound data collection instruments.

While such activities are beyond the scope of this manual, additional information can be found in the citations at the end of this chapter. Assistance may also be available from your state library or regional library cooperative system.

Step 5: Study the Information

Now the most challenging part of Looking Around begins. Again, both staff and planning committee have an important role. The library staff organize and present the results of the information-gathering activities to the planning committee. The planning committee then translates this new knowledge into a form useful for decision making.

Organizing the Information

At this stage, the results, or findings, of the library's information-gathering activities are largely unorganized. The next task of the staff who gathered the information is to determine how best to organize the information for presentation to the planning committee. In general, group information items in a way that will simplify interpretation and use. Several schemes for organizing the information are possible.

- *Service orientation:* Relate information items to selected library services. Information items that apply to more than one service may appear several times.
- *Roles orientation:* Libraries that used roles (see Chapter 4) to focus information gathering may use those same roles to organize the information gathered. Again, information items relevant to more than one role may be restated with each role.
- *Topical outline:* Use the general scheme presented in Workform C (see Figure 7), or, if major trends are evident, organize the information in terms of these changes in the library's community or services.

Try looking at the information from several different points of view. Group and regroup the information. Break down figures in alternative ways. For example, try looking at circulation per hour open or dollar spent on materials per day. It is not necessary to interpret the information at this stage, but the information should be presented to the planning committee in a clear, logical manner. This facilitates an orderly review of the information and helps the planning committee keep its attention on the most important findings.

Interpreting the Information

Now that the information has been gathered and organized, the planning committee must decide what this information means. It translates the findings into needs, opportunities, and library decision areas. This process is not a straightforward matter. A description of "what is" does not lead directly to clear-cut agreement about "what should be." Interpretation is a complex task calling for reflection and judgment. The findings focus discussion, but the committee will need to think both analytically and creatively about the meaning and implications of the findings.

Workform D, Translating the Findings of Looking Around (see Figure 9), can assist the committee in this process. The committee may spend one or more meetings discussing the findings and recording their conclusions. As the planning committee uses Workform D, they:

- List in capsule form each of the major findings
- Note briefly how this finding might impact library services—either in terms of the current situation or the potential for change
- Given these impacts, determine if there are any opportunities or circumstances implied by the findings that the library should exploit
- Consider how the library might respond to the findings.

WORKFORM D Translating the Findings of Looking Around

Major Finding	Impact on Library Roles and Services?	Opportunities?	Possible Library Responses?
1.			
2.			
3.			
etc.			

FIGURE 9 Reduced Workform D: Translating the Findings of Looking Around

During the discussion, some general points should be kept in mind. First, both factual and subjective information are important. The impressions and opinions of individuals must be combined with "hard" data, such as population statistics or economic information. Subjective information places factual data in perspective, and factual data challenges or substantiates subjective impressions.

Second, watch for surprises. Some information may confirm staff or committee impressions of "the way things are." Other information may, however, challenge long-held assumptions. Such areas should be reviewed carefully. They may indicate areas where change is especially needed.

Third, try to place all information in perspective. Sometimes, to interpret statistics about the library's performance (such as circulation per capita or document delivery figures), it may be helpful to know what is possible. Such statistics may have more meaning if they are compared to the library's past performance or to statistics from similar libraries.

Fourth, libraries that have conducted surveys should remember that surveys are not ballots. The planning committee, director, and board are not honor bound to act directly on individual survey items. Often those responding are not aware of all the facts or constraints under which library services are provided. The opinions and perceptions of library users and the community at large are useful in planning, but not binding.

Workform D provides a foundation for concluding this planning phase and for continuing the planning process. Chapter 4, Developing Roles and Mission, uses the findings as the planning committee considers which roles are most crucial for successfully meeting community needs for library service. As the library moves further ahead in the planning process, the "Opportunities" column of Workform D may suggest areas for goals and objectives (Chapter 5), and the "Possible Library Responses" column may suggest specific activities for implementation (Chapter 6).

Step 6: Report the Results

Finally, the results of Looking Around are summarized. This summary serves as a permanent record for the current committee and for future committees. The length, complexity, and format of the report varies with the library's level of effort. Libraries reporting at a basic level of effort can use a "cleaned-up" version of Workform D to transmit the results of Looking Around to subsequent planning phases. For these libraries, Workform D will become a key source document for the final planning document (see Chapter 7).

Libraries Looking Around at a moderate or extensive level of effort may produce a more lengthy report. Figure 10 suggests the basic content for such a report and can be modified to match your library's needs. Suggestions for adapting this outline by level of effort are provided in the level-of-effort box accompanying Step 1. General guidelines for the report are:

- Begin with a brief executive summary giving an overview of the report's contents
- Keep the language and tone of the report simple, clear, and direct
- When reporting statistical data, rely on tables, pie and bar charts, and other visuals (individually numbered and titled) rather than lengthy paragraphs that simply list numbers or percentages
- Explain the implications and importance of each chart, table, or summary presented
- Have someone knowledgeable about the library but *not* involved in Looking Around review the report to make certain it is readable and understandable.

The library has now examined its external environment and internal conditions. This Looking Around has resulted in a statement of key findings which have been discussed and interpreted by the planning committee. These findings, their potential impact, the opportunities noted, and possible library responses provide input for the next planning phase, Developing Roles and Mission (Chapter 4), and for the planning phases to follow.

Sources for Additional Information

Busha, Charles H., and Stephen P. Harter. *Research Methods in Librarianship*. New York: Academic Press, 1980.

Chapter 3 provides an overview of the techniques and principles involved in survey design and administration. Chapter 6 reviews additional research methods including observation, case studies, library user studies, library and community surveys, etc.

Executive Summary

- Summarize in one or two pages the basic findings, their meaning, use in the planning process, and the overall value of the process.

Introduction

- State the general focus for the Looking Around process: what did the library want to find out?
- Describe how the Looking Around process was managed and over what time period.

Approach

- What Looking Around activities were accomplished?
- Briefly report what procedures and existing sources of information were used, what agencies were contacted, and what other methods were used to gather information.
- How were data collection instruments, if any, developed?
- Explain how the information was analyzed.

Findings

- State the findings, and present summary tables. Organize the findings by broad topics (such as the roles described in Chapter 4), major library service or program areas, or by the results from particular Looking Around activities.
- Give an overview of what the findings mean, how they impact library services and operations, and discuss the implications of the findings for library planning.

Appendixes

- Copies of any data collection instruments used.
- Support documents for Looking Around such as time schedules, explanation of statistical procedures used, etc.
- Any other materials, such as maps, that might be useful in explaining the Looking Around process.

NOTE: To be used for moderate or extensive level of effort only.

FIGURE 10   Suggested Outline for Reporting the Results of the Looking Around Process

Dillman, Don. *Mail and Telephone Surveys: The Total Design Method.* New York: Wiley, 1978.

Although its cost data is outdated, this invaluable work provides step-by-step details for how to conduct successful mail and telephone surveys. It contains numerous checklists and examples helpful to the novice.

Epstein, Irwin, and Tony Tripodi. *Research Techniques for Program Planning, Monitoring, and Evaluation.* New York: Columbia University Press, 1977.

Libraries interested in structured observation may wish to review Chapter 5, Using Observational Techniques for Planning Staff Training Programs. This chapter discusses the principles of structured observation, applies those principles, and cites a specific application as an example.

Gallup Organization, Inc. *Book Reading and Library Usage: A Study of Habits and Perceptions.* Princeton, N.J.: The Gallup Organization, Inc., 1978.

This publication is an example of studies in the library literature that explore patterns in reading and library usage.

Hernon, Peter, and Charles R. McClure, editors. *Microcomputers for Library Decision Making.* Norwood, N.J.: Ablex Press, 1986.

Useful chapters for libraries intending to use microcomputers during Looking Around, include Chapter 6, Designing a Spreadsheet Decision Support System in a Library, and Chapter 12, Microcomputers for In-house Data Collection and Research.

McClure, Charles R., Douglas L. Zweizig, Nancy A. Van House, and Mary Jo Lynch. "Output Measures: Myths, Realities, and Prospects." *Public Libraries* (Summer 1986): 49—52.

The article gives an overview of the issues involved in determining what quality of information is appropriate for use in library management, and gives suggestions for interpreting measures data.

Palmour, Vernon E., Marcia C. Bellassai, and Nancy V. De Wath. *A Planning Process for Public Libraries.* Chicago: American Library Association, 1980.

Part III, Collecting and Using Data, discusses surveying as a method for gathering planning information. Examples of surveys for staff, citizens, students, and library users are presented along with suggestions for tabulating and analyzing the results.

Swisher, Robert, and Charles R. McClure. *Research for Decision Making.* Chicago: American Library Association, 1984.

Libraries interested in gathering original data through surveying or sampling will find this publication useful. Chapters 3–5 discuss research design, data gathering, and sampling.

U.S. Bureau of the Census. *County and City Data Book, 1983.* Washington, D.C.: Government Printing Office, 1984.

This publication combines a wide variety of social and economic data from Census Bureau publications. Most information is available by state, county, city, and standard metropolitan statistical areas.

Van House, Nancy A., Mary Jo Lynch, Charles R. McClure, Douglas Zweizig, and Eleanor Jo Rodger. *Output Measures for Public Libraries.* Second edition. Chicago: American Library Association, 1987.

This publication provides a useful overview of the basic principles for surveying and sampling, such as usefulness, validity, reliability, precision, comparability, etc. It gives basic procedures for deriving the output measures referenced in this chapter and suggests approaches for reporting, interpreting, and using measurement data.

Developing Roles and Mission

Libraries reflect the diversity and character of the communities they serve. Excellence in library service is not a simple matter of numbers. It lies in the "fit" between the library's roles and the needs and expectations of the community it serves. As communities change, so do their libraries.

This chapter introduces a set of basic service roles and explains how these roles and the library's mission statement are linked. By using the results of Looking Around to select roles and define a mission statement, the planning committee can state, "For *this* community and for *this* planning cycle, *this* is what the library will be." That statement frames decisions to come in later planning phases: Writing Goals and Objectives (Chapter 5) and Taking Action (Chapter

6). This chapter describes five basic steps:

1. Determine level of effort
2. Study library roles
3. Select library roles
4. Prioritize library roles
5. Write the mission statement.

Developing roles and mission may occur at this point in the planning process, or it may be completed prior to Looking Around as a basis for determining which information to collect. In the sequence presented here, the planning committee can take advantage of the results of Looking Around to help it determine the library's current performance with respect to the roles and the availability of critical resources to support each role.

Public Library Roles

Public library roles are profiles of library service emphases. Taken as a group, they provide a catalog of library service images. Each role is a shorthand way of describing a combination of factors important in planning:

• What the library is trying to do
• Who the library is trying to serve
• What resources the library needs to achieve these ends.

Figure 11 introduces eight library roles. These roles (described in more detail later in this chapter) provide a menu for selecting the roles most appropriate for your library's circumstances. No library has a large enough budget, staff, or collection to meet *all* the service needs of its community. No library can fulfill all roles with excellence, so each library must focus its resources on a *limited* number of roles.

The notion of limitation may be uncomfortable. Yet choices about service priorities not made deliberately are made by default. Librarians make choices on a daily basis. Taken in-

dividually, these choices often seem small. Which book to buy? Which item to catalog first? Whether to add a microcomputer for public use or to recarpet the children's area? The effect of such decision making is, however, cumulative. These choices define the library. They determine where the budget is spent and how staff spend their time.

By selecting which roles to emphasize, the planning committee provides criteria for making these decisions. The planning committee and library staff need to balance their vision for desired roles with a clear recognition of which roles the library can realistically fulfill. These roles become the focus for library resources and energies during the years ahead. Stating these choices explicitly allows the library to:

• Relate services to identified community needs and library conditions
• Concentrate on the most needed service areas
• Communicate service priorities to staff, local government, and the public
• Allocate resources more effectively.

The roles presented in this chapter are generalizations, not absolutes. They encompass most public library contributions to a community, but do not describe all possible library services. Divisions between roles are a matter of judgment. Some roles overlap to a certain extent, and some library activities apply to more than one role. If your library is selecting roles at an extensive level of effort, you may identify or define roles unique to your library's circumstances. However, the standard set of roles presented in Figure 11 is useful for comparative purposes.

Public Library Mission

The mission statement is a concise expression of the library's purpose. It specifies the fundamental reasons for the library's existence. In this sense, it builds on, but is not limited to, the roles chosen by the library. The mission establishes the scope of the library's activities for the current planning cycle and acts as a foundation for other planning phases. In one sense, the mission is like a job description: it gives direction to the library's daily activities.

Brief, simple, and direct, the mission is especially well-suited to communicating with the public. It concentrates the essence of the library's role choices in nontechnical language and communicates the library's "business" to

---

Community Activities Center: The library is a central focus point for community activities, meetings, and services.

Community Information Center: The library is a clearinghouse for current information on community organizations, issues, and services.

Formal Education Support Center: The library assists students of all ages in meeting educational objectives established during their formal courses of study.

Independent Learning Center: The library supports individuals of all ages pursuing a sustained program of learning independent of any educational provider.

Popular Materials Library: The library features current, high-demand, high-interest materials in a variety of formats for persons of all ages.

Preschoolers' Door to Learning: The library encourages young children to develop an interest in reading and learning through services for children, and for parents and children together.

Reference Library: The library actively provides timely, accurate, and useful information for community residents.

Research Center: The library assists scholars and researchers to conduct in-depth studies, investigate specific areas of knowledge, and create new knowledge.

FIGURE 11   Public Library Roles

Level of Effort for
Developing Roles and Mission

Basic

The library director and the planning committee devote one meeting to reviewing the roles and their components, linking the roles to the results of the library's Looking Around activities, completing the role selection exercise, and prioritizing the roles. Roles are selected on a library-wide basis. The planning committee uses Workform F (see Figure 16) to brainstorm ideas for the mission statement. The director or another staff member drafts the statement for approval by the committee.

Moderate

The director and planning committee spend at least one meeting reviewing the roles and discussing the implications of the roles in terms of the results of Looking Around and the library's resources. Key staff and the library board also participate in the role selection exercise. A separate planning committee meeting is scheduled to review the results of the role selection exercise on a group by group basis, discuss the composite results, and prioritize the roles. The planning committee and key staff use Workform F (see Figure 16) to brainstorm ideas for the mission statement. A staff person prepares a draft mission statement which may be reviewed by the library board and staff prior to receiving approval from the planning committee.

Extensive

The planning committee obtains input from a wide variety of groups (general library staff, elected officials, the community, the library board) as it selects roles. Central library/branch roles may be selected in addition to library-wide roles. The planning committee allots a series of meetings to study the roles, explore their ramifications in terms of library resources and community needs, to assess variations in point of view demonstrated by the different groups involved in the role selection exercise, to finalize their role selections, and to rank the roles. The planning committee encourages input from staff, board, and other interested groups in brainstorming the mission statement. A staff person prepares a draft mission statement which is reviewed widely. The draft statement may go through several reviews before adoption by the planning committee.

staff, elected officials, and the community at large. In contrast, the role descriptions are most useful to the staff, board, and planning committee. Because they are lengthy, the roles require more thought, time, and study to "digest." However, the roles and the role selection process help library staff to set priorities, to define the library's mission, and to direct daily library activities.

With each new planning cycle, the planning committee tests the role choices of the previous cycle and evaluates the mission statement. If the roles and mission statement still reflect the li-

brary's purposes and service priorities, they stand for the next cycle. If not, they are rewritten to reflect changing circumstances.

Step 1: Determine Level of Effort

In addition to the general factors affecting level-of-effort choices and your library's interest in this planning phase, the planning committee faces two additional considerations: establishing organizational relationships for the role selection process and selecting participants in the role selection process.

Participants in the Role Selection Process

Role selection provides an excellent opportunity to involve a variety of groups in the library's planning activities. Because selecting library roles is influenced by values as well as by objective consideration of the library's circumstances, diversity of viewpoint is healthy. The planning committee may ask the library staff (collectively or by organizational unit), board of trustees, local government officials, or community groups to complete the role selection exercise (Step 3). The results from these groups are reported to the planning committee for review, comparison, and discussion. Increasing the number of groups participating in the role selection exercise increases the level of effort for this planning phase.

Organizational Relationships in the Role Selection Process

Public libraries with branches have several choices for coordinating role selections among the branches and the library as a whole. Options include:

• Library-wide roles only
• Central library/branch roles in addition to library-wide roles
• Central library/branch roles only, but in the context of a library-wide mission statement.

In making this decision, consider how your library plans to set goals and objectives. For example, if you plan to set library-wide goals and objectives, roles may also be chosen for this level. If separate goals and objectives are established for individual library units, then roles may be appropriate for these units as well. (See Chapter 5 for more detail.)

If your library decides to develop both library-wide and central library/branch roles, the planning committee must decide what sequence to use for role selection. Developing library-wide roles first provides guidance for branches, but may limit their vision. Developing branch roles first may ignore overall library priorities. Either sequence is workable. The choice is largely a matter of management style. However, increasing the number of units selecting roles increases your library's level of effort proportionally.

Step 2: Study Library Roles

The planning committee's study of library roles has two parts: reviewing the roles and their components, and linking the roles to the results of Chapter 3, Looking Around. The amount of time spent on studying the roles varies with your library's level of effort for this planning phase.

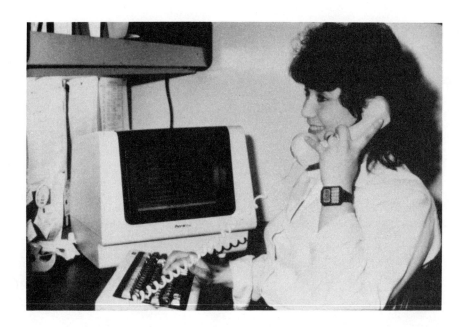

Reviewing the Roles and Role Components

A thorough understanding of the eight basic library roles lays the foundation for the role selection process. Each role has four components: Description, Benefits, Critical Resources, and Output Measures to Explore.

Description highlights the service aspects of the role—what is done and for whom. Service examples are provided to illustrate the range of activities associated with each role. In some cases, suggestions for ways to focus the role by subject or clientele group are given.

Benefits from a particular role can accrue both to individuals and to the community. This component briefly describes some of these advantages and suggests possible political implications for selected roles.

Critical Resources are factors that significantly affect the library's ability to fulfill each role. These resources are grouped under the headings of collection, staff, and facilities. Generally, resources should already be in place to support the roles your library will emphasize during the current planning cycle. If resources are absent or weak, success in fulfilling the roles chosen depends on how quickly needed resources can be acquired.

The last role component is *Output Measures to Explore.* Judging a library's degree of success in achieving a role is a complex process, one in which a professional body of knowledge is still emerging. Determining success requires combining experience, judgment, and objective measurement. A wide variety of evaluation techniques can be applied to each of these roles.

As a starting place for your exploration, however, this manual lists measures described in *OMPL,* second edition. The "Further Possibilities" discussion for each measure in that manual suggests additional analyses of the data collected, options for additional data collection, and supplementary measures. These suggestions can help you tailor measures associated with the library's roles to meet your evaluation needs more precisely. As you use these measures and other evaluation techniques during the planning process, keep these points in mind.

- No single measure tells a complete story. Interpret performance measure scores in context with each other, with other evaluation techniques you are using, and with the library's overall service program.
- Performance measure scores are not absolutes. There are no "right" or "wrong" scores for performance measures. Interpret performance measure scores in context with your library's role profile and mission.
- Exercise patience in working toward improving performance measure scores. Changing your library's score on a set of measures is not done overnight.

Role Descriptions

The next section of this chapter presents eight basic library roles. It has been designed to allow the reproduction and distribution of these pages to role selection participants.

Community Activities Center

DESCRIPTION: The library is a central focus point for community activities, meetings, and services. It works closely with other community agencies and organizations to provide a coordinated program of social, cultural, and recreational services.

The library provides both meeting room space and equipment for community- or library-sponsored programs. Programs might include book talks, health information fairs, book discussion groups, community issues forums, speaker series, concerts, art exhibits or humanities programs. The library may be a source of programming for local cable television. Library facilities may be used for organizations providing health testing programs, tax assistance, youth groups, voter registration, and the like.

BENEFITS: Community members have opportunities to explore their common heritage, discuss their divergent views on issues and current topics, and receive some social services. The library enhances the attractiveness of the community by providing a central location for cultural, civic, and recreational activities. Since co-operation and co-sponsorship with other community organizations are central to this role, the library develops an effective communication network. This network supports the library in carrying out other roles it has selected.

CRITICAL RESOURCES: *The collection* is not emphasized in this role.

The staff have wide, direct involvement in many community organizations. They promote community activities and act as liaisons between the library and community groups.

The facility is central to this role. It might include an audiovisual production lab, cable TV studio, give-away racks, display facilities, teleconferencing facilities, or community bulletin boards. In some instances, the library may share facilities with other community agencies. The building is easily accessible, has adequate parking, and contains enough meeting rooms and informal space to accommodate a variety of functions.

OUTPUT MEASURES TO EXPLORE:
• Library Visits Per Capita
• Program Attendance Per Capita

Community Information Center

DESCRIPTION: The library is a clearinghouse for current information on community organizations, issues, and services. The library maintains a high profile as a source of information about community services. It responds to community problems with specialized services provided both inside and outside the library building, such as a job information and skills center for a community with high unemployment.

The library may create local directories, maintain files of local organizations and service agencies, or index local newspapers. The library participates in community referral networks, and maintains and publicizes a master calendar of community events. The library participates with other agencies in planning programming or information fairs on community issues such as drug abuse and teenage pregnancy.

BENEFITS: Users have a one-stop center to obtain current information about community organizations, issues, and services. Access to this information helps individuals to become self-sufficient, control their lives, and better understand community issues. For the community, the library helps link those in need of services and resources with an appropriate provider. This role puts the library in the communication network of the community and helps identify the library as part of the community decision-making process. In considering this role, the library must be aware of potential competition for this role from other agencies, and must clarify the library's role in relation to these groups.

CRITICAL RESOURCES: *The collection,* in addition to regular reference materials, contains locally developed files with data on community agencies, clubs, and interest groups. The library has extensive vertical files on issues of current public interest and subscribes to local newspapers and the newsletters of local agencies and organizations. The library uses online services to supplement local information resources.

The staff are skilled in reference and referral interviewing techniques, knowledgeable about community resources and services, and are competent in organizing and maintaining locally constructed files and indexes. The staff are active in the community, participate in community organizations, and keep abreast of local issues.

The facility has an adequate number of telephone lines. Ample meeting room space and

parking space are available to support the library's programming activities.

OUTPUT MEASURES TO EXPLORE:
• Library Visits per Capita
• Program Attendance per Capita
• Reference Completion Rate
• Reference Transactions per Capita.

Formal Education Support Center

DESCRIPTION: The library assists students of all ages in meeting educational objectives established during their *formal* courses of study. This may include students in elementary and secondary schools, colleges, community colleges, universities, or technical schools, as well as those involved in training programs, literacy or adult basic education, and continuing education courses. This emphasis on registration for formal instruction distinguishes the Formal Education Support Center from the Independent Learning Center.

The library offers tours for classes and instructs students on using library tools. It may sponsor a homework service using qualified volunteers to assist students with assignments. In cooperation with local schools, the library may reserve special materials to meet classroom assignment needs. It may develop a clearinghouse to identify providers of formal education and training or may support a literacy program. To assist faculty, the library may supply supplementary print and audiovisual material for classroom use.

Libraries emphasizing this role may specify the educational levels supported (for example, elementary and secondary, but not postsecondary).

BENEFITS: Users find materials to supplement what is available in school or academic libraries, and can use the library to identify providers of education and training. The library is an alternative study site when school or academic libraries are crowded, inconvenient, or unavailable. This role closely associates the library with education, and benefits taxpayers by supplementing, not duplicating, other educational collections. Since this role involves cooperation, the public library must exercise initiative in clarifying its role and initiating cooperative collection development with other institutions.

CRITICAL RESOURCES: *The collection* contains materials in all formats and at levels appropriate to the educational level(s) supported by the library. Resources include reference materials, periodicals, abstracting and indexing services, online databases, and access to interlibrary loan. The library may make a special effort to acquire materials listed as supplemental sources in textbooks used by local education providers.

The staff are knowledgeable about educational programs in the community and work closely with local educators. At least some staff are knowledgeable about curriculum needs and educational principles.

The facility is easily accessible, has ample parking, and may be located near a formal educational institution. The building has quiet space and carrels for individual study, typing facilities, or microcomputers with word processing software for students to use in completing school assignments. The library is open for a broad range of hours to meet student needs.

OUTPUT MEASURES TO EXPLORE: (Calculate these measures using student population figures.)

• In-Library Materials Use per Capita
• Reference Completion Rate
• Subject and Author Fill Rate
• Title Fill Rate.

Independent Learning Center

DESCRIPTION: The library supports individuals of all ages pursuing a sustained program of learning independent of any educational provider. These individuals set their own learning objectives to meet such concerns as citizen education, self-improvement, job-related development, hobbies, and cultural interests. The staff help learners identify an appropriate learning path, determine needed resources, and obtain those resources from the library's collection or through interlibrary loan. Continuing, intensive staff involvement or counseling with individual learners is a distinguishing characteristic of this role.

The library may function as an educational information center providing occupational counseling or learning/skill inventory tools to help individuals assess their needs. Other services may include a learning exchange, linking individuals with others offering to teach a skill, or providing adult programs on high-interest learning topics, such as nutrition. Staff may assist children with interests outside the school curriculum, such as pets, rock or stamp collecting, or dinosaurs. They may prepare "pathfinders," self-help research guides on selected topics, and help learners identify a customized sequence of study materials.

Libraries may focus on specific subject areas or on special age groups.

BENEFITS: Users can pursue self-determined and self-paced study on various subjects. Independent learners use the resources of the library to "get ahead," to do better in their work,

to clarify their values, to learn something new, or to adjust to changes in life and work, such as moving to a new community or retiring. The library supports an educated, self-reliant, and productive citizenry, thus contributing to the stability, attractiveness, and economic well-being of the community. Citizens who use the library can be powerful allies.

CRITICAL RESOURCES: *The collection* has a wide range of circulating subject materials relevant to the interests of independent learners of all ages. The materials are in a variety of formats and geared to varying levels of ability. Some libraries develop extensive collections of audio or video cassettes on popular self-help topics such as health issues, investment planning, home repair, foreign languages, and psychology.

The staff are knowledgeable about learning theory, general educational principles, and local opportunities for educational and training programs. They are skilled in assisting independent learners and capable of developing self-guided materials for introducing learners to various subjects.

The facility is easy to use with minimal staff assistance, has good signage, comfortable reading areas, and some space set aside for quiet study and for staff to counsel with learners. The library is conveniently located and open for a broad range of hours.

OUTPUT MEASURES TO EXPLORE:
- In-Library Materials Use per Capita
- Title Fill Rate
- Subject and Author Fill Rate.

Popular Materials Library

DESCRIPTION: The library features current, high-demand, high-interest materials in a variety of formats for persons of all ages. The library actively promotes and encourages the use of its collection.

Merchandising techniques, such as face-out shelving, displays, or paperbacks near the checkout area, may be used within the library. Special booklists may be distributed or materials gathered together to encourage circulation in connection with a library program, such as a children's story hour, summer reading program, or a young adult program. The library may circulate materials at off-site outlets, such as shopping malls or community facilities. For residents in the community with limited access to library facilities, the library may include popular materials in its services to jails, nursing homes, etc.

Libraries selecting this role may specify age groups or formats to be emphasized.

BENEFITS: A wide variety of popular materials for reading, listening, and viewing are available to library patrons. Since some individuals purchase these materials, the library returns an economic benefit to those who borrow, rather than buy, such items. This role enhances and supplements the offerings of community bookstores, theaters, video outlets, and media. The library's support for cultural and leisure activities makes the community an inviting place to live in and visit. Providing popular materials contributes to a high circulation rate. This, in turn, leads to high visibility for the library in the community.

CRITICAL RESOURCES: *The collection* includes current and popular materials in a variety of formats, with sufficient duplication to meet demand. A substantial percentage of the collection has been published within the past five years.

The staff are knowledgeable about current popular interests and anticipate publishing trends and "hot" titles.

The facility promotes browsing, has attractive displays and good signage. The building has adequate and easily accessible shelf space, provides casual seating, is in an easily accessible site, and has ample parking.

OUTPUT MEASURES TO EXPLORE:
• Turnover Rate
• Browsers' Fill Rate
• Subject and Author Fill Rate
• Title Fill Rate
• Circulation per Capita
• Registration as a Percentage of the Population.

Preschoolers' Door to Learning

DESCRIPTION: The library encourages young children to develop an interest in reading and learning through services for children, and for parents and children together. Parents and other adult caregivers can locate materials on reading readiness, parenting, child care, and child development. Cooperation with other child care agencies in the community is ongoing.

The library promotes reading readiness from infancy, providing services for self-enrichment and for discovering the pleasures of reading and learning. Services may include programs for infants, for parents and toddlers, and for parents— for example, "read-aloud," day-care story hour, traditional storytelling, parenting skills development workshops, and booktalks. The library may provide outreach to day-care facilities, or reading readiness programs. Programming introduces children and adults concerned with children to a wide range of materials and formats.

BENEFITS: Preschoolers have a place designed for their needs with trained adults to help them satisfy their curiosity, stimulate new interests, and find information. They become familiar with library materials in a variety of formats and develop reading, listening, viewing, and thinking skills. Parents can obtain resources and services to support their efforts to develop their children's interests, experience, knowledge, and development.

For the community, the library promotes early reading and acceptance of reading, factors contributing to successful performance in formal schooling. This role promotes lifelong use of the library and contributes to the library's image as an educational center for individuals of all ages. This role generates visibility, popularity, and support for the library in the community by reaching children unserved by any other community agency. In addition, services for children are popular with voters.

CRITICAL RESOURCES: *The collection* has a variety of materials and formats for preschoolers and for adults working with young children. Some libraries provide computers, audiovisual formats, educational toys, and games to help children expand their imagination and develop motor and sensory skills. Popular titles are available in multiple copies.

The staff are knowledgeable about early childhood development and children's litera-

ture and promote reading readiness to the community. They guide children's choices of books and other materials and are skilled in planning and conducting programs.

The facility is in a location easily accessible to young children. Ample, inviting space is available for programs and story hours. Shelving and furnishings are attractive, accessible, and comfortable for young children.

OUTPUT MEASURES TO EXPLORE: (Use the percent of the population under 5 for per capita measures. For turnover rate, use only the portion of the collection intended for use by preschoolers, such as picture books and audiovisual materials.)

• Circulation per Capita
• Library Visits per Capita
• Program Attendance per Capita
• Turnover Rate.

Reference Library

DESCRIPTION: The library actively provides timely, accurate, and useful information for community residents in their pursuit of job-related and personal interests. The library promotes on-site and telephone reference/information services to aid users in locating needed information. Information provided may range from answering practical questions (how to remove garden pests, what to feed a guinea pig, how to apply for a job, what is the name of a poem that starts with . . .), to specialized business-related research (finding patent information), to answering questions about government (locating regulations for a grant program), to providing consumer information. The library participates in interlibrary loan and cooperative reference services to meet patron needs for information not available locally.

Libraries selecting this role may identify subject areas of particular strength or emphasis.

BENEFITS: Library users have convenient, timely access to information needed for daily living and decision making. They can find out about almost any subject and obtain materials not generally available elsewhere. Such a library contributes to local economic development by strongly supporting the information needs of businesses and strengthens local government by providing information for policy formulation and program management.

CRITICAL RESOURCES: *The collection* emphasizes informational materials to support individual, business, government, and community interests. Materials are available for all ages and reading levels. The reference collection is extensive and includes such material as indexes, atlases, encyclopedias, handbooks, and directories. The library makes heavy use of electronic databases and has a large current periodicals collection. The library may maintain subscriptions to special indexing and abstracting services and keep files on area businesses. Development of local history archives and collecting local documents, memorabilia, and photographs may also be emphasized.

The staff are approachable and skilled in using reference tools and reference interviewing techniques. Collectively, the staff have strong subject backgrounds in the library's areas of subject strength.

The facility has a clearly identified and visible location for reference and information services that is staffed during all hours of library service. An adequate number of telephone lines are available for telephone reference and online database searching.

OUTPUT MEASURES TO EXPLORE:
• Reference Transactions per Capita
• Reference Completion Rate
• In-Library Materials Use per Capita.

The Research Center

DESCRIPTION: The library assists scholars and researchers to conduct in-depth studies, investigate specific areas of knowledge, and create new knowledge. The library's collection, generally developed over a long period of time, is a source of exhaustive information in selected subject areas (historic, cultural, scientific, or social). The library engages in this role as a result of tradition, community expectations, or state library agency plans, and is likely to be a net-lender for interlibrary loan activity. It may make special services available to scholars and other researchers, such as assigned carrels and lockers, customized database searching services, or operation of a photocopy center.

A library choosing this role should specify the subject disciplines in which it intends to be a Research Center. For example, in a city with major glass fabrication industry the public library may maintain a research collection in such areas as glass chemistry or art glass.

BENEFITS: Scholars intensively pursue intellectual and professional interests using locally owned materials. Additional materials are obtained through resource-sharing networks. The community is identified as a center for research and knowledge, making it an attractive place for professionals who need easy access to extensive information resources. This role gives the library a unique value in the community.

CRITICAL RESOURCES: *The collection* has a large number of titles, extensive serials holdings, microform materials and equipment, a wide array of printed and electronic abstracting, indexing and database services, and may include archival and manuscript materials. A high percentage of the collection in subject areas pertaining to the library's research specialties contains material that is scholarly, theoretical, or technical in nature.

The staff are likely to have advanced degrees in subject disciplines, to understand research methodologies, and are knowledgeable about the literature in their field of emphasis.

The facility has adequate space to house the library's extensive collection, a photocopy center, quiet study areas, and carrels. The library may also have a conservation laboratory for the preservation of fragile or rare materials.

OUTPUT MEASURES TO EXPLORE:
• Title Fill Rate
• Reference Completion Rate
• In-Library Materials Use per Capita
• Document Delivery.

Linking Roles with Looking Around

Now the planning committee applies the understanding it developed during Looking Around to the set of library roles. By thoughtfully and creatively relating library conditions, community characteristics, and current trends to the roles, each committee member develops an opinion about which combination of roles is most appropriate for your library. There are no clear, one-to-one links between any single piece of information and a particular library role. Each role, however, suggests a service atmosphere and resource needs; and the collective findings of Looking Around suggest service needs and library strengths and weaknesses.

As resources for this review, use the workforms developed in Chapter 3: Workform D, Translating the Findings of Looking Around; (see Figure 9); Workform C, Options for Library Planning Information (see Figure 7); and the library's formal report of its Looking Around activities. During committee discussion, the following questions may be helpful:

• Which roles, regardless of their current emphasis in library programs, seem to respond best to community needs identified during Looking Around?
• To what extent does your library have the critical resources associated with each role? If resources are inadequate, can they be increased?
• What does your library's performance, as indicated by selected output measures or library service statistics, indicate about its capacity to meet certain roles?
• Which roles have the greatest potential for increasing the visibility, importance, or integration of the library in the community?

Step 3: Select Library Roles

The planning committee is now ready to select roles for the library. This step has two major activities: completing the role selection exercise and discussing the results of the exercise. To gain broader input, the planning committee may ask additional groups (such as staff, library board, or friends of the library) to participate in this exercise. These groups should receive an orientation to the roles. Several approaches are possible:

• Distribute role descriptions for participants to read and discuss in advance

• Orally review the roles with participants just prior to the exercise
• Devote a full meeting to introducing and discussing the roles.

The Role Selection Exercise

To complete the role selection exercise, the planning committee and other participant groups in role selection use Workform E, Selecting Library Roles Worksheet (see Figure 12). Color-code these forms for different groups, or enter the name of the group on the form to allow results for each group to be tabulated separately. This exercise helps those who participate to:

• Consider the appropriateness of each role for the library
• Communicate their perceptions of current library services
• Communicate their view of appropriate future library roles.

Each participant individually completes Workform E by dividing points among the roles in two ways. First, points are allocated among current activities. How does each person perceive current library services and priorities? Second, points are allocated among the roles on the basis of how each person feels library priorities should be weighted. Differences between the two columns (Current Activities and Desired Commitment) give the planning commit-

WORKFORM E Selecting Library Roles Worksheet

_____
(Group)

In the columns below, please allocate 100 points. You need not divide points equally, and some roles may receive no points. Note that 20 of the 100 points have already been assigned to cover basic library activities and roles not selected for emphasis. In the first column, distribute the 80 remaining points based on how you see *current* library activities being directed. In the second column, distribute the 80 points the way you feel library activities *should* be directed.

Role	Current Activities	Desired Commitment
Community Activities Center		
Community Information Center		
Formal Education Support Center		
Independent Learning Center		
Popular Materials Library		
Preschoolers' Door to Learning		
Reference Library		
Research Center		
Miscellaneous Activities and Roles Not Selected for Emphasis	20	20
Total	100	100

FIGURE 12 Reduced Workform E: Selecting Library Roles Worksheet

Group: **Morningside Library Planning Committee**

For both current activities and desired commitment, enter in the appropriate box the total number of points given to each role by all participants in the group. Divide the total by the number of participants in the group to obtain the average for each role. Rank the roles from 1 to 8, with a 1 ranking attached to the role with the highest average score.

Role	Current Activities			Desired Commitment		
	Total Points	Average Score	Rank	Total Points	Average Score	Rank
Community Activities Center	24	3	7	24	3	7
Community Information Center	48	6	6	64	8	5
Formal Education Support Center	104	13	4	144	18	1
Independent Learning Center	80	10	5	120	15	3
Popular Materials Library	112	14	3	56	7	6
Preschoolers' Door to Learning	144	18	1	96	12	4
Reference Library	120	15	2	136	17	2
Research Center	8	1	8	0	0	8
Miscellaneous Activities and Roles Not Selected for Emphasis[1]	160 (8×20)	20	x	160 (8×20)	20	x

[1] For miscellaneous activities, multiply the number of persons in the group by 20, and enter the result in the total boxes.

FIGURE 13   Sample Role Selection Tabulation Sheet (Results from a Planning Committee of Eight)

tee a sense of where change may be needed.

After each participant group has completed Workform E, the results for each group are tabulated separately and reported to the planning committee. Figure 13 is an example of a report from a planning committee of eight. Scores from each individual have been totaled, the results averaged, and, for ease of reference in discussion, a rank number has been assigned. If different groups participated (for example, board members, staff, and community), results from each group can be compared. Such comparisons can provide valuable input for the committee's deliberations.

Discussing the Results of the Role Selection Exercise

After the results of the role selection exercise have been compiled, the planning committee determines which roles are most important for the library. They begin by considering the following questions:

• What roles have similar ratings for current activities and desired commitment? Which roles show large differences?
• What roles are appropriate for the library, given the community's characteristics, information needs, or other data identified in Looking

Around—even if those roles are not currently emphasized by the library?

- Are critical resources available for the roles with the highest total and average scores?
- Does the library's performance indicate that more emphasis is currently placed on some roles rather than others?
- If the Role Selection Total Sheet was distributed to different groups, how do their rankings compare? Are obvious differences apparent in the ratings given to current services or those proposed for desired commitment? If differences are noted from group to group, why?
- If the library has branches, do central library/branch role selections seem in harmony with each other and with library-wide role selections?
- How similar are the roles with the highest averages and totals to the library's current service profile?
- Does orienting any of the roles toward a particular subject area, material format, or clientele group seem appropriate or necessary given the library's circumstances?

The goal of this discussion, which should encourage a lively exchange of viewpoints, is to develop a consensus on which two to four roles are most important for the library. Arriving at this agreement is not merely a simple process of adding "votes." The planning committee must balance the complex set of factors implied by the questions above to arrive at their conclusions. If discussion has been lengthy or involved, the planning committee may repeat the role selection exercise. This allows committee members to incorporate new ideas gained during the discussion.

At the conclusion of this step, the planning committee has agreed upon the two to four roles of central importance for the library. The final number of roles selected depends on the size of the library and on the staff energy and financial resources available to channel into implementing the roles.

Step 4: Prioritize Library Roles

The planning committee now assigns role priorities by placing each role into one of three categories: primary, secondary, or maintenance. The roles chosen for emphasis at the conclusion of the role selection exercise become primary or secondary roles. Approximately 80% of the library's effort is directed toward the primary and secondary roles (see Figure 14). This com-

mitment cannot be translated directly into library budget dollars. The fixed and continuing costs associated with operating the library will continue to consume most of the library's budget. Rather this commitment represents:

- The direction of planning committee attention—for example, primary and secondary roles become focal points for Writing Goals and Objectives (Chapter 5) and for Taking Action (Chapter 6)
- The concentration of staff energy—for example, as the results of the planning process are implemented, the staff uses the priorities implied by the primary and secondary roles to guide their activities
- The redirection of at least some library resources—for example, the budget for collection development may be realigned as a result of role choices.

Roles not chosen for emphasis become maintenance roles. The remaining 20% of the library's effort supports these roles and other miscellaneous library activities. Maintenance does not mean that a role will be cut off or ignored. However, it does mean that such a role will not be developed during the remainder of the planning process or serve as the focus of new library initiatives. Nor will such a role receive a major commitment of library resources or staff energy. The library's response to such a role is passive rather than active.

To determine which of the two to four roles selected for emphasis should become primary and which secondary, the planning committee discusses the following questions:

- What patterns were evident in the totals and averages as roles were selected? Did one or two roles clearly stand out, or were the top roles fairly evenly ranked?
- Which roles respond to the greatest community need?
- Which roles are best supported by the library's critical resources?
- Which roles are most compatible with each other?
- Which roles represent the greatest change for the library?

After this discussion, the planning committee should reach a consensus on which roles are primary, which secondary, and which maintenance for the duration of the planning cycle. Primary and secondary roles will receive special emphasis as the library prepares its mission statement during the next step.

Level of Priority	Large Libraries or Libraries with Extensive Resources	Branch/Small Libraries or Libraries with Moderate Resources	Effort/Commitment Level
Primary	1–2 Roles	1 Role	40%–50%
Secondary	1–2 Roles	1–2 Roles	30%–40%
Maintenance Level	Remainder of Library Roles and Activities	Remainder of Library Roles and Activities	20%

FIGURE 14   Recommended Number of Role Priorities

Step 5: Write the Mission Statement

The planning process is like a funnel. The beginning of the process is like the wide end of the funnel, open to all kinds of possibilities. As planning decisions are made, the funnel narrows. In selecting and ranking roles, the planning committee has begun to narrow the library's priorities for service and to concentrate library strengths. The preparation of the mission statement is a vital continuation of this process.

The mission statement expresses briefly and directly the library's purpose and service priorities for the current planning cycle. As noted earlier, it builds on, but is not limited to, the roles chosen for emphasis. The mission is a more creative expression of the primary and secondary roles, capturing their spirit without being tied to the exact wording of the role descriptions used in this chapter. It is important, however, to preserve clearly the identity and focus of the roles chosen. The mission statement implies criteria for evaluating the library's overall performance and, by implication, it indicates areas the library will not emphasize. Primary and secondary roles are given more or less emphasis in the mission statement to reflect their priority. Figure 15 gives an example.

The final wording of the mission statement is best assigned to a single individual. However, the planning committee can effectively provide direction to the writer by suggesting ideas or by providing draft phrases and statements. These suggestions can be communicated using Workform F, Drafting the Mission Statement (see Figure 16). If desired, Workform F can be completed separately for each primary and secondary role. The basic steps are:

• Review the descriptions of roles selected for primary and secondary emphasis

• Identify key words and phrases
• Brainstorm additional words or phrases that express the ideas the committee wishes to emphasize
• Record suggestions in the appropriate category on Workform F
• Transmit the results to the individual responsible for drafting the mission statement.

The categories shown on Workform F should stimulate thinking. If Workform F is used in a group setting, results can be recorded on a flipchart. If planning committee members complete the form individually, the results are collected and given to the individual writing the mission statement. If Workform F has been completed separately for each primary and secondary role, the writer of the mission statement will have many forms and suggestions to draw upon in drafting a mission statement for committee review and final approval.

The planning committee has selected primary and secondary roles for emphasis during the planning cycle and has adopted a concise mission statement. These products provide a framework for the next planning phase, Writing Goals and Objectives.

Roles Selected: Primary: Formal Educational Support Center and Reference Library. Secondary: Preschoolers' Door to Learning and Independent Learning Center.

Mission Statement: The Morningside Public Library provides materials and services to help community residents obtain information meeting their personal, educational, and professional needs. Special emphasis is placed on supporting students at all academic levels and on stimulating young children's interests and appreciation for reading and learning. The library serves as a learning and educational center for all residents of the community.

FIGURE 15   Sample Mission Statement

WORKFORM F   Drafting the Mission Statement

Most mission statements have common elements. In the space below, jot down a few sentences or phrases that capture your understanding of the library's mission for the role(s) indicated and your personal perspective. Check whether the role designated is a primary or secondary role for your library.

Role: _____   Primary Role: _____

Secondary Role: _____

Mission Statement Elements

Who:
Needs:
Concepts:

Who: People in the community, children, young adults, seniors, families, library users, library nonusers, students, independent learners, ethnic groups, the institutionalized, etc.

Needs: Recreational, leisure, informational, educational, cultural, social, historic, civic, intellectual, etc.

Concepts: Access to information, meeting users' needs, reaching new users, reaching nonusers, interlibrary cooperation, intellectual freedom, public awareness of library services, linking people with ideas, stimulating intellectual life, preserving cultural and intellectual heritage, helping individuals solve daily practical problems, etc.

FIGURE 16   Reduced Workform F: Drafting the Mission Statement

Sources for Additional Information

Bolt, Nancy and Corinne Johnson. *Options for Small Public Libraries in Massachusetts: Recommendations and a Planning Guide.* Chicago: American Library Association, 1985.

Although the role descriptions vary slightly from those in this manual, pages 35 through 50 present an approach for relating critical resources to library roles. Libraries wishing to explore this aspect more fully in the role selection process may find these pages useful.

Dubberly, Ronald A. "Why You Must Know Your Library's Mission." *Public Libraries* (Fall 1983): 89–90.

This article discusses the importance of developing a library mission statement and notes the dynamic nature of the mission statement as it responds to changes in the community and the needs of library users.

Martin, Lowell. "The Public Library: Middle-age Crisis or Old Age Crisis." *Journal Library* 108 (January 1, 1983): 17–22.

This landmark article introduces the concept of roles for public libraries and argues persuasively that libraries must make choices based on their communities and resources.

Public Library Association. Goals, Guidelines, and Standards Committee. *The Public Library Mission Statement and Its Imperatives for Service.* Chicago: American Library Association, 1979.

By presenting a far-ranging and broad overview of the place of the public library in society, this brief publication can provide valuable background information for the planning committee to use in defining the concepts most crucial to your public library's unique mission.

Writing Goals and Objectives

5

After developing roles and a mission statement, the planning committee writes goals and objectives. Goals and objectives are not established in a vacuum. They are based on information developed during the planning steps described in Chapters 3 and 4 and the intuition and common sense of those involved in the planning process. The goals and objectives should:

- Support the roles and mission statement (Chapter 4)
- Respond to community characteristics and information (Chapter 3)
- Consider the presence or absence of library resources (Chapter 3).

The goals and objectives must be linked to the roles and mission statement. This linking can be encouraged by maintaining some overlap between those involved in the roles and goals/objectives-setting processes.

The purpose of this chapter is to assist the planning committee in writing goals and objectives. It explains the importance of goals and objectives, identifies some factors that should be considered before writing them, and offers a set of steps to follow in writing goals and objectives.

Writing goals and objectives is as much an intuitive, creative process as it is a set of steps to follow. However, the following steps will be discussed for writing goals and objectives:

1. Determine level of effort
2. Review existing information
3. Generate and screen goals
4. Generate and screen objectives
5. Make objectives measurable
6. Write draft set of goals and objectives
7. Rank objectives
8. Review the final goals and objectives statements.

Importance of Goals and Objectives

Goals and objectives are essential in the planning process because they identify areas of activity most important for the library and establish targets of performance within those areas. More specifically, goals and objectives:

- Guide the actions of decision makers
- Inform the community and library staff about what service activities the library will emphasize
- Aid the library in assessing its performance and demonstrating accountability
- Provide a basis for developing activities and tasks (see Chapter 6).

With a clear statement of goals and objectives the library can state explicitly the most important activities and performance targets during the planning cycle.

What Are Goals and Objectives?

Goals are long-range, broad, general statements describing a desired condition or future toward which the library will work during the next 3–5 years. Goals can be expressed from either the library's or public's viewpoint. They should flow logically from the roles and mission statement and provide a framework for setting objectives.

Objectives are short range and describe the results to be achieved in a specific time period. They are measurable, doable, time limited, begin with an action verb, and are more specific than a goal. Accomplishing objectives helps the library fulfill its goals, roles, and mission.

Types of Goals and Objectives

Public library goals generally fall into the following categories:

- *Service goals:* These goal statements relate directly to the library's roles and stress the services that the library intends to provide to its clientele. An example of a service goal is: library clientele are provided with accurate and timely reference assistance.
- *Management goals:* These goal statements relate to resources, facilities, staffing, funding, or other managerial matters. These goals may support service goals. An example of a management goal is: the library has adequate and modern physical facilities to house its materials.

In practice, a single goal may include aspects of each category. However, thinking of goals in this manner may be useful for generating goal statements.

Objectives typically are written for each goal but may relate to more than one goal. They may be of the following general types:

- *Developing new services or operations:* for example, to establish three new outreach programs for young adults during the current fiscal year.
- *Maintaining or improving the quality of an existing service or operation:* for example, to increase title fill rate to 65% by the end of the current fiscal year.
- *Eliminating or minimizing existing problems:* for example, to reduce the number of library materials stolen this calendar year by 10%.

Figure 17 shows examples of service and management goals with objectives for each.

Preparing to Write Goals and Objectives

The planning committee should consider several factors prior to writing goals and objectives. Together, these factors offer a broad set of options from which the planning committee can "customize" the process of writing goals and objectives to fit your library's particular situation.

Goals and Objectives within the Larger Planning Cycle

The planning cycle is typically a 3–5 year time period. Usually, the library roles, mission, and goals stay the same throughout this period. Objectives, however, are typically established for shorter periods of time, usually 1–2 years. Thus, the planning cycle includes a number of objectives cycles as shown in Figure 18.

For a library doing planning the first time, goals, objectives, activities, and tasks are developed. After the activities are implemented and reviewed (Chapter 6), the library establishes another set of objectives for the next objectives cycle. But reviews in the objectives cycles do not revise the goals, roles, and mission statement.

At some point during an objectives cycle (usually 3–5 years after the original planning cycle was initiated), the library director or the planning committee determines that revision of the roles, mission statement, and/or goals

---

SERVICE GOALS

Goal 1: Members of the community are able to obtain materials and services to pursue their own learning and meet their individual information needs.

    Objectives:

    a. to obtain the use of three meeting room facilities outside the library for adult independent learning programming.
    b. to increase adult attendance per capita for programs related to self-improvement by 25% by the end of fiscal year 19__.

Goal 2: Community children and young adults have access to a wide range of high quality services.

    Objectives:

    a. to increase young adult annual library visits per capita by 40% by June 30, 19__.
    b. to provide reading readiness programs to a minimum of 250 preschoolers during the current fiscal year.

MANAGEMENT GOALS

Goal 3: The library recruits, trains, and retains the most competent personnel available.

    Objectives:

    a. to develop an annual performance evaluation process for all library staff by June 30, 19__.
    b. to increase the number of full-time professional staff to 8 by June 30, 19__.

Goal 4: The community is well-informed about library services.

    Objectives:

    a. to obtain an assessment of the community's awareness of library adult services by June 30, 19__.
    b. to increase registration as a percentage of population to 40% by June 30, 19__.

FIGURE 17 Example Goals and Objectives for Morningside Public Library

should occur. This signifies the end of the current planning cycle and the start of Reviewing Results (see Chapter 8).

Some directors schedule the objectives cycles to coincide with the annual budgeting process. That is, objectives are developed to assist in planning the next year's budget and making budget requests. This approach may be easier to manage, but library managers should take care that financial concerns do not limit creativity and innovation when generating objectives.

Organization for Writing Goals and Objectives

The library has a number of options when organizing for writing goals and objectives. The director may draft preliminary goals and objectives for review by the planning committee. The planning committee may develop goals and objectives itself, or it may establish a subcommittee to conduct the process. Or, additional staff and/or community involvement in the process is possible. The key issues are to clarify responsibility for this planning phase and to consider the level of effort that can be committed to this process.

As suggested in Chapter 2, Planning to Plan, a planning chart (Figure 4) can (1) identify tasks to be accomplished and methods to be used in developing goals and objectives, (2) determine who will be responsible for each task, and (3) establish the sequence of tasks over time. Using such a chart to plan for writing goals and objectives is a good idea.

Options for Relating Roles, Goals, and Objectives

Each library must determine for itself the relationship among its roles, goals, and objectives. There are a number of options depending on the management style of the director, experience of the library staff in developing goals and objectives, the characteristics of the community, and the organizational complexity of the library.

SINGLE LIBRARY WITH NO BRANCHES

One option is to develop goals and objectives for the library as a whole. Objectives are likely to cut across individual departments. A second option is to use the library goals to write objectives organized by departments or functional areas within the library. This approach may identify activities easier to implement than those that cut across library departments. A third op-

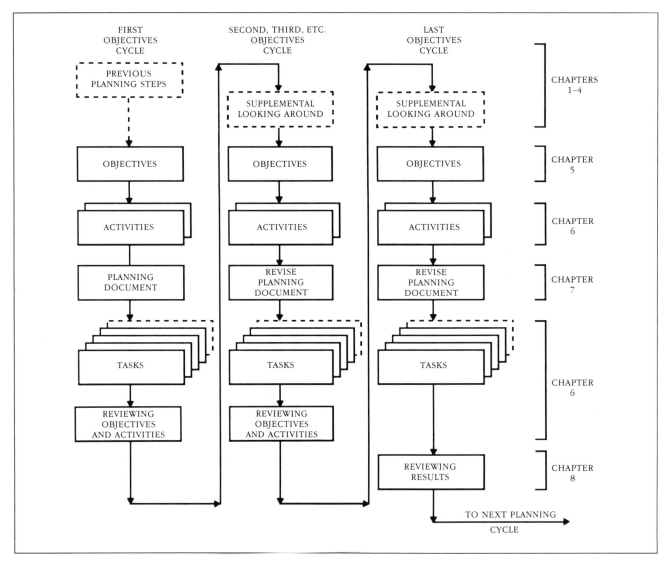

FIGURE 18 The Objectives Cycle

tion is for the library to combine the above two approaches.

LIBRARIES WITH MULTIPLE OUTLETS

In this situation, the structure and relationships among roles, goals, and objectives can vary widely. Possible options include:

• *Library Roles and Mission, Library Goals, and Central Library/Branch Objectives:* the library as a whole develops roles, mission, and goals. Each of the branches and the central library then develops objectives. Branch objectives are completely dependent on library roles, mission, and goals.

• *Library Roles and Mission, Library Goals, Branch Goals, and Central Library/Branch Objectives:* roles, mission, and goals are estab-

lished for the library, but the branches also establish goals and objectives. Such an approach provides a degree of interdependency as well as independence for the central library and the branches.

• *Library Mission, Branch Roles, Branch Goals, and Central Library/Branch Objectives:* in this structure, greater independence is given to the branches and the central library to respond to unique service area conditions allowing them to specify their own roles, goals, and objectives.

There are no hard and fast rules for which approach is "best." The director and the planning committee should discuss possible structures and determine which best suits their library.

For a library with multiple outlets, the planning committee may also need to consider the coordination and balance among:

- Objectives related to internal operations, departments, and procedures versus service objectives
- Roles, goals, and objectives related to individual branches and each branch's community information needs, versus library-wide roles, goals, and objectives
- Headquarters' roles, goals, and objectives which may stand by themselves versus those that serve primarily to support the branches.

Depending on the framework agreed upon, procedures for writing goals and objectives (described later in this chapter) may have to be modified. For example, a planning committee for a library with multiple outlets might choose to have library-wide goals and branch objectives. Branch librarians may develop branch objectives which the planning committee can coordinate library-wide.

Guidelines for the Number of Goals and Objectives

In the first planning cycle, it is important to develop only a few goals and objectives. This approach will help the planning committee and library staff be successful in accomplishing the objectives and developing a positive attitude toward planning. The first planning cycle is a learning process. In later cycles, staff will have a better sense of how many goals and objectives can be realistically developed and implemented.

Generally, then, planning committees with limited experience writing goals and objectives or those completing this phase at a basic level of effort probably should write no more than 5–7 goals. For each goal, probably no more than 1–2 objectives during each objectives cycle should be written. Increased numbers of goals and objectives may be appropriate for libraries with greater planning experience. Avoid the temptation of writing goals and objectives that cover "everything" the library does and intends to do. You should concentrate only on those goals and objectives that are most important for this particular planning cycle.

Sequence for Writing Goals and Objectives

When developing goals and objectives for the first time, you may use either of two basic approaches:

- Establish goals first, then objectives
- Establish goals and objectives together in an interactive process.

The first approach is described in this manual and is more commonly used. Generally, the larger the library, the more branches, and the more complex the organizational hierarchy, the more likely that a first, separate process will be needed to develop goals, and then another to write objectives. During the second objectives cycle (see Figure 18), only objectives will be generated.

Step 1: Determine Level of Effort

You can write goals and objectives quickly or you may take a good deal of time. The process can include much or minimal library review and discussion. Consider how much time participants may need and how much time is available. Consider also the factors discussed in the previous section as they also will affect the level of effort. Remember that writing goals and objectives is an ongoing, cyclic process. Each review of the goals and objectives will make them better. This fine-tuning, however, may take place over a number of years.

Typically, the planning committee has responsibility for writing goals and objectives. However, many different individuals or groups may be involved in the process:

- Library management, which is responsible for overseeing the process
- Library staff, who may contribute to the writing and review process
- Governing boards, which review the results of the process
- Individual citizens, who may suggest particular goals at open hearings regarding possible library activities
- Consultants—either from the state library or elsewhere—who may help those involved in library planning.

As the number of people involved in the goal and objective setting process increases, so do the amount of time required and the extent of library resources necessary to complete the process.

Step 2: Review Existing Information

Before setting goals, the planning committee reviews the results of Looking Around (Chapter

Level of Effort for
Writing Goals and Objectives

Basic

This level accommodates the needs of libraries with limited resources and time. It relies heavily on the director's ability to draft goals and objectives that reflect the needs/interests of the community and the resources available to meet those needs.

Based on information from earlier phases of the planning process, the director and/or the planning committee drafts a set of goals and objectives. The objectives may be based on output measures. The objectives are measurable by inspection or by use of the measures in *OMPL,* second edition. After some additional review and discussion, the director and/or the planning committee writes a final set of goals and objectives.

Moderate

The planning committee spends additional time generating and discussing goals and objectives. Library staff may become involved in goals and objectives development and may participate in brainstorming sessions held with the planning committee regarding their particular areas of expertise. For example, when goals and objectives for children's services are being developed, the children's librarian might participate in the discussion.

Staff might also participate in the ranking and reviewing of the goals and objectives. Staff participation can be obtained by selecting certain key individuals by areas of the library, for example, reference services, or by branch libraries—if present. Measurement techniques for the objectives rely primarily on output measures and less on inspection.

Extensive

If the library has branches serving a diverse and/or rapidly changing population, or is facing a radically altered funding situation, writing goals and objectives may require additional attention. The number and type of goals and objectives can be increased. Discussions can be held as to writing unique patterns for goals and objectives within the library or library system. Customized measures described under "Further Possibilities" in *OMPL,* second edition, may be necessary to assess the objectives. Detailed attention can be given to coordinating and relating goals and objectives across the branches. A number of discussions and revisions of the goals and objectives may be necessary.

Community members may work with the planning committee, staff, or library board in identifying and writing goals and objectives. The Friends of the Library (if available) may be a means to obtain the names of interested citizens who will be willing to participate in this process.

3) and Developing Roles and Mission (Chapter 4). In general, the planning committee reviews the current status of the library: projects already "in the works"; needs, interests, and trends within the service area; and the likelihood of stable, increased, or decreased funding in the foreseeable future. Perhaps most importantly, committee members augment this review with vision, creativity, and good judgment. In addition, consider these questions:

• Which roles did the library choose as most appropriate and why?
• Which library services are currently being targeted at which audiences? Are these still appropriate?

- Which services are perceived as most significant by library staff and library clientele? Do these perceptions match? Why or why not?
- What library services are most appropriate for the community and for the chosen roles?

Step 3: Generate and Screen Goals

The library director, a member of the planning committee, or a staff member might develop a list of possible goals as a basis for discussion. The list is a first attempt and the author should recognize that others will revise it later. This approach is useful because it often is easier for others to generate goals from a preliminary set of ideas. At this stage, those generating the goals need not be overly concerned about specific wording.

A second approach is brainstorming. This is an informal process for sharing ideas. The planning committee or other participants generate ideas at random about possible library goals. Generally, the brainstorming process works as follows:

- Make certain participants in the brainstorming process have basic information about the library such as roles and mission statement.
- A group leader discusses types of goals, and explains the difference between goals and objectives (see discussion above).
- A group leader may offer a preliminary list of goals as a basis for discussion.
- Encourage participants to generate as many ideas regarding goals as possible. The more ideas produced the better. Three different but related perspectives for generating ideas are:

  Roles perspective: Relate key areas of the roles selected for emphasis by the library to potential services and audiences. Determine what ideal conditions would exist if the roles were to be fulfilled.
  Community perspective: Review the results from Looking Around (Chapter 3). Identify significant community groups (children, the aging, racial minorities, etc.) and list goals from the perspective of these groups.
  Library resources perspective: Review the critical resources required for the roles (Chapter 4). Identify significant library weaknesses (collections, services, programs, staff, etc.) and list possible goals. Such needs, however, should be consid-

ered in light of their impact on meeting community information needs.

- Record these ideas on newsprint pads or a blackboard.
- Allow no one to evaluate, criticize, or defend any of the goal ideas until the brainstorming session is over.
- Then, discuss the relative strengths and weaknesses of the goals produced during the brainstorming session, including such questions as:

  What factors may affect these goals and to what degree can the library control those factors?
  What value are these goals to (1) individuals using the library and to (2) the community at large?
  What can be done realistically by the library to promote the development of each goal?
  To what degree do these goals support the roles and mission statement?

- Maintain a record of the discussion of the goals and their strengths and weaknesses.
- Limit the goals to a manageable number. This can be done by the planning committee after the brainstorming session by ranking the relative importance of the goals.*

This approach operates on the principle that several heads are better than one in making judgments about possible goals.

A final statement of goals can now be produced and, if desired, reviewed one more time by the planning committee. One person, however, should be responsible for producing these "polished" goal statements.

Regardless of how the goals are generated, the result is a preliminary list of goals, each of which should:

- Describe an ideal condition or state that the library believes important for fulfilling its roles and mission statement
- Be stated in a declarative sentence
- Be free of library jargon
- Provide a framework for objectives during the next 3–5 years.

In summary, the goals should be short, concise, and easily understood by both library staff and community members.

---

*Ranking can be done by a point allocation process similar to that described in the ranking of roles (see Figure 13) or by a more general assessment such as that described in the ranking of objectives (see Figure 21).

Step 4: Generate and Screen Objectives

In practice, this step may be done at the same time as the next step, Making Objectives Measurable. Sometimes the planning committee may decide on an objective and then search for an appropriate measure. Or, sometimes, the planning committee may agree that a particular output measure is important and develop an objective based on that output measure. Appendix A lists output measures discussed in *OMPL,* second edition, which can assist you in this process.

In other instances, the director or a member of the planning committee may generate a preliminary draft of possible objectives for discussion. If the library has multiple outlets, librarians in the branches may participate in the process. Or, the planning committee may wish to brainstorm possible objectives (as described in the previous step for generating goals).

Objectives Based on Output Measures

Some libraries may already have collected output measure data either for Looking Around or through previous work with *OMPL,* first or second edition. Based on this information, they may wish to concentrate their attention on a particular library activity related to the output measures.

If libraries do not have output measure data, they may still wish to establish objectives based on output measures. For example, let's assume that the planning committee is concerned about access to the collection as measured by title fill rate. With this output measure in mind, they can then establish an objective: to obtain a title fill rate of 55% by June 30, 19__.

Figure 19 summarizes typical library service areas and suggests output measures that might be used as a basis to develop objectives for those areas. These output measures (as well as others) are described in greater detail in *OMPL,* second edition.

Criteria for Objectives

Regardless of the approach taken, the planning committee should make certain that when reviewing the objectives, each of the following questions can be answered with a "yes":

- Is the objective related to at least one goal?
- Does the objective begin with an action verb, for example, *to provide, to increase, to establish, to conduct,* etc.?
- Is the objective an end and not a means to an end?
- Does the objective include a date by which it will be accomplished?
- Does the objective specify "what" and "when" and not discuss "why" and "how"?
- Does the objective take advantage of a situation or condition that will benefit the library or its community?
- Is the objective measurable or verifiable, that is, how will librarians know if the objective has been achieved?
- Does the objective specify a *single* result to be accomplished?
- Are there a number of different ways in which the objective could be accomplished?
- Is the objective "actionable," that is, is it realistic that the library can develop activities to accomplish this objective?
- Is the objective understandable and written clearly and simply?

Library Service Area	Possible Output Measures
Library Use	Library Visits per Capita Registration as a Percentage of the Population
Materials Use	Circulation per Capita In-Library Materials Use per Capita Turnover Rate
Materials Access	Title Fill Rate Subject and Author Fill Rate Browsers' Fill Rate Document Delivery
Reference Services	Reference Transactions per Capita Reference Fill Rate
Programming	Program Attendance per Capita

NOTE: Explanation of these measures and suggestions for developing additional measures can be found in *OMPL,* second edition.

FIGURE 19 Output Measures for Typical Library Service Areas

Further, it is useful to ask yourself, "what will be different for the user or member of the community as a result of this objective?" This question focuses attention on developing a "results-oriented" perspective.

Step 5: Make Objectives Measurable

The criterion "is the objective measurable?" is especially important and deserves additional attention and discussion. Measurable objectives are essential for effective planning because they provide:

- Ongoing evaluation of how well implementation is progressing
- A basis to make comparisons between current, previous, and future performance levels
- A summary assessment of the success with which objectives are accomplished.

Quantitative and Non-quantitative Measures

To know when an objective has, in fact, been accomplished, either a quantitative or non-quantitative measure is used. Quantitative measures are preferred, but sometimes there is no readily available quantitative measure for a particular objective.

Output measures are an excellent way to provide a quantitative assessment of an objective. They are especially appropriate to use for objectives linked to service-type goals. They can assess three possible dimensions of services:

- *Quantity:* These measures reflect the amount of service provided, often standardized in some way for the service or need. Circulation per capita, for example, measures the quantity of books loaned for the population served.
- *Quality:* These measures reflect the "goodness" or effectiveness of the service provided. Title fill rate, for example, is the proportion of patron title searches that were successful, that is, the user's chance of success in finding materials or the quality of the library's collection.
- *Responsiveness:* These measures reflect how rapidly services are delivered. Document delivery time, for example, reflects how long a user has to wait for materials not on the shelf when a request is made.

However, other types of measures can also be used to measure an objective. *Input measures* include reference staff hours, size of collection, materials budget, etc. *Productivity measures* reflect the efficiency with which resources are used. They compare the quantity of resources used to the quantity (and sometimes quality) of service provided using those resources. These types of measures may be more appropriate for use with objectives linked to management-type goals.

It is also possible to use a nonquantitative means to determine if an objective has been accomplished. The technique most frequently used is "by inspection." For example, objective "a" of goal 3 on Figure 17 "to develop an annual performance evaluation process by June 30, 19__," is verified by inspection. Either the process was or was not developed by June 30, 19__.

However, there are weaknesses when using a non-quantitative approach. For example, staff cannot determine *the degree* or quality to which the objective has been accomplished. Thus, there may be disagreement about the *extent* to which the objective was, in fact, accomplished. Whenever appropriate, output measures should be used to determine the degree to which an objective is accomplished. However, it is better to use other types of measures than to use no measure!

Criteria for Measures

When developing measures for objectives, the following criteria should be kept in mind:

- *Validity:* Is the measure providing an assessment of the activity desired or could it be measuring something else?
- *Reliability:* Are the data used for the measure sufficiently accurate and consistent?
- *Relationship to roles:* Does the measure assist the planning committee assess how well the library is fulfilling its roles (see Chapter 4)?
- *Affordability:* Can the library afford the resources necessary to produce and analyze data for a particular measure?
- *Sensitivity:* Will the measure accurately reflect changes in activities being measured? For example, a library that does very little interlibrary loan may find that document delivery time varies considerably from one period to the next. Such may be true because a few requests in a short period have a major effect on the measure.

These criteria (and others discussed in *OMPL*, second edition) should be used for assessing the appropriateness of a particular measure *and* to determine the level of effort to be committed when developing measures.

Workform G, Assessing the Measurability of an Objective (see Figure 20), is intended to assist planners determine the "measurability" of an objective. Each objective can be assessed by the criteria suggested on the workform. Additional criteria can be added if desired. If the objective cannot be easily measured, it may need to be modified or eliminated.

WORKFORM G   Assessing the Measurability of an Objective

Objective 1: _____

_____

_____

1. What is the measure for this objective? _____

_____

2. What data will be needed for the measure? _____

_____

3. What are the procedures for obtaining the data? _____

_____

_____

4. How easily can these procedures be implemented and the data obtained?

_____

_____

5. To what degree are adequate staff time and other resources present to collect and analyze the data?

_____

_____

_____

Objective 2: _____

_____

_____

. . . repeat questions 1–5 above, and continue for each objective.

NOTE: If responses for each of the questions on this workform cannot be provided, the objective should be revised or abandoned.

FIGURE 20   Reduced Workform G: Assessing the Measurability of an Objective

WORKFORM H   Ranking Objectives

_____

Instructions: Please indicate your assessment of the overall importance of each objective listed below. Write in the right-hand column the number that represents your assessment of that objective based on the following code:

5 = Essential: Must Be Done! Find   3 = Important: Should Be Done If   1 = Desirable: Do If Time and
    a Way of Funding   Possible   Funds Allow.

Objective and Rationale	Rank

Objective 1: _____   _____

_____

[Rationale If Available] _____

_____

Objective 2: _____   _____

_____

[Rationale If Available] _____

_____

Objective 3: _____   _____

_____

[Rationale If Available] _____

FIGURE 21   Reduced Workform H: Ranking Objectives

Step 6: Write Draft Set of Goals and Objectives

Generally, it is best to assign one person on the planning committee or the library staff the responsibility of producing the draft set of goals and objectives. Basically, this person "polishes up" the results of Steps 3 and 4. During this process, some librarians have found it useful to include a rationale for each objective. For example, an objective and rationale might look like this:

Objective: to increase adult program attendance per capita by 20% during the current fiscal year.

Rationale: The percentage of adults in the community has increased significantly during recent years and there are few opportunities in the community for adults to attend educational and cultural programs. Further, this objective will assist our library in fulfilling its role of Community Activities Center.

Inclusion of a brief rationale for each objective statement helps in the ranking process (next step) by offering some insight into why this particular objective is important. Further, it serves as another check on the objective. If a rationale cannot be stated, perhaps the objective is inappropriate or needs to be fine-tuned. At the completion of this step, the planning committee has a draft statement of goals and objectives.

Step 7: Rank the Objectives

The process for ranking objectives depends, in part, on the level of effort being dedicated to writing goals and objectives. Ranking may be performed by an individual or a committee. Generally, the more people involved in the ranking process, the greater the level of effort. On the other hand, the more people involved, the greater the likelihood that participants will understand and be committed to implementing the objectives.

One approach is for the planning committee to rank each objective as "essential," "important," or "desirable." This method, based on Workform H (see Figure 21) simplifies the process of obtaining consensus from participants. You can give a score to each objective as a basis for ranking its overall importance.

After the ranking occurs, the planning committee reviews the results. Committee members, for example, may decide to accept the two most highly ranked objectives for each goal. Or, the committee may wish to develop their own rules for how many and which objectives will be accepted. Regardless, there should be at least one objective for each goal, and it is important that only the most important objectives are accepted.

Libraries with multiple outlets may need to coordinate rankings among branches. If branch librarians conduct their own ranking process, the rankings can be submitted to the planning committee. The planning committee can review and coordinate the ranked objectives and make certain that (1) the branch goals and/or objectives support library roles, goals, and mission statement, and (2) the branch goals and/or objectives are mutually supportive and not mutually competitive.

This step results in a ranked list of objectives. This list of the most important objectives should be combined with the list of goals to produce a final statement of goals and objectives such as that shown in Workform I (see Figure 22).

Step 8: Review the Final Goals and Objectives Statement

The statement of goals and objectives should be reviewed one last time to assess its overall appropriateness, political impact, or other factors. This review can be conducted by the planning committee and/or the director, or it may include selected staff and members of the board. It is a final check to make certain that (1) the goals and objectives are, in fact, realistic and (2) there are no unforeseen political implications or consequences of the goals and objectives.

An additional benefit from the review is that it may provide increased understanding and commitment to the goals and objectives. The better you understand the goals and objectives, the more likely you can translate the objectives into activities and tasks (see next chapter).

The result of these eight steps is a written statement of the library's goals and objectives. The actual format of this statement may vary from that shown in Workform I (see Figure 22) depending on the configuration of roles, goals, and objectives agreed upon for the library.

Depending on the management preferences of the director, the statement of goals and objectives may be submitted to the library board (or other appropriate governing body) for approval. Or, the director may decide to submit

WORKFORM I, Part A   Summary of Roles, Goals, and Objectives for Library without Multiple Outlets

Primary Library Roles: Level of Commitment: 50%
　　　Role 1: _____
　　　Role 2: _____
Secondary Library Roles: Level of Commitment: 30%
　　　Role 3: _____
　　　Role 4: _____
Remainder of Library Roles and Activities   Level of Commitment: 20%
　　　　　　　　　　　　　　　　　　　　　　　　　　　　　　　　　　　　100%
Mission Statement: _____

Goal 1: _____

　　Objective 1.1: _____

　　Objective 1.2: _____

Goal 2: _____

　　Objective 2.1: _____

　　Objective 2.2: _____

WORKFORM I, Part B   Summary of Roles, Goals, and Objectives for Library with Multiple Outlets
(Assuming the planning committee has agreed that branches have branch roles, goals, and objectives.)

Branch Name: _____ Date _____
Mission Statement for the Library: _____

Primary Library Roles: Level of Commitment: 50%
　　　Role 1: _____
　　　Role 2: _____
Secondary Library Roles: Level of Commitment: 30%
　　　Role 3: _____
　　　Role 4: _____
Remainder of Library Roles and Activities   Level of Commitment: 20%
　　　　　　　　　　　　　　　　　　　　　　　　　　　　　　　　　　　　100%
Branch Goal 1: _____

　　Objective 1.1: _____

　　Objective 1.2: _____

Branch Goal 2: _____

　　Objective 2.1: _____ . . . and so forth

NOTE: The library should list the appropriate number of goals and objectives as agreed upon from the ranking process (see Workform H).

FIGURE 22   Reduced Workform I: Summary of Roles, Goals, and Objectives

an entire planning document for approval rather than only the goals and objectives (see Chapter 7).

Although the writing of goals and objectives is an essential step in the planning process, in and of itself it will not cause change to occur. During the next step, Taking Action, you translate the objectives into activities and tasks, and the planning process begins to have tangible impacts on services and operations.

Sources for Additional Information

"ALA Strategic Long-Range Plan." *American Libraries* 17 (June 1986): 462–463.

This planning document provides examples of goals stated in terms of ideal conditions. It may provide a useful illustration of the format and style for goal statements.

Anthony, William P. *Practical Strategic Planning.* Westport, Conn.: Greenwood Press, 1985.

Pages 87–88 describe a process, "Nominal Group Training," that can be used effectively with brainstorming for generating and ranking goals and objectives.

Van House, Nancy A., Mary Jo Lynch, Charles R. McClure, Douglas Zweizig, and Eleanor Jo Rodger. *Output Measures for Public Libraries.* Second edition. Chicago: American Library Association, 1987.

This manual provides excellent guidance for developing and using output measures. It is an especially important reference source when developing measures for objectives.

Zweizig, Douglas L. "Tailoring Measures to Fit Your Service: A Guide for the Manager of Reference Services." *The Reference Librarian* No. 11 (Fall-Winter 1984): 53–61.

Customizing measures for particular services will be done primarily at an extensive level of effort. This source offers suggestions for how this customizing process can be done in a reference services context. The suggestions, however, can be used to develop measures in other service areas of the library.

Taking Action

6

Taking Action is one of the most exciting steps in the planning process. The necessary ingredients for successfully Taking Action are vision, creativity, ability to exploit opportunities, and an innovative approach to accomplishing the library's objectives.

In this phase of the planning process, the planning committee and staff translate the library's objectives into activities and tasks. An activity is a set of tasks that accomplish an objective. A task is a specific action that must be done to implement an activity. Tasks describe *how* an activity is implemented. Taking Action has these major steps:

1. Determine level of effort
2. Identify possible activities to accomplish each objective
3. Select activities
4. Change the planning perspective

5. Manage implementation
6. Monitor the implementation process
7. Review objectives and activities.

The first three steps are "getting ready." Step 4 is making the transition from thinking about implementation to doing it; Steps 5 and 6 both describe how implementation is managed; and Step 7 is a review process. Linking objectives to activities is not simply a matter of taking steps—the process also requires creativity and pragmatism.

For roles, goals, and objectives, the planning process emphasized "ends," or where the library should be and what it should be doing. But now, the process focuses on "means," or how the library reaches those ends. Thus, moving from objectives to Taking Action requires a pragmatic mindset rather than the philosophical one required earlier.

Step 1: Determine Level of Effort

At this phase of the planning process, responsibility for planning shifts from the planning committee to the director and the library staff. Although the planning committee may participate in identifying and selecting activities, library staff implement those activities. Thus, staff involvement throughout this planning phase is essential.

A number of options for organizing this phase are possible. For example, the director may develop possible activities and obtain feedback from key staff. The planning committee may ask for additional staff participation, especially for specifying tasks. Or a small staff committee might suggest activities for review by the director and planning committee. Regardless of the approach, establishing clear lines of responsibility increases the success of implementation.

Activities are likely to be most effective when designed in the context of existing library responsibilities and projects. An important consideration is matching staff skills to these activities and tasks. The director should consider: what staff skills or strengths exist? what are existing staff workload levels? The director and planning committee must be sensitive to these factors as activities are developed, selected, and implemented.

For each of the steps described in this chapter, you can commit a different level of effort. For example, an extensive level of effort may be committed to Step 2, Identifying Possible Activities, but a basic level of effort might be committed to Step 6, Monitoring the Implementation Process. The planning committee can consider which level of effort is appropriate for each step after reading through this chapter. Suggestions for determining level of effort are provided in the box, "Level of Effort for Taking Action."

Step 2: Identify Possible Activities

There are many ways to accomplish any given objective. In this step, you will identify several possible activities for each of the library's objectives. This will help you make certain that the best activities are selected for implementation.

This step should be approached creatively. Those involved in this step should consciously note opportunities for activities in the library, the community, or the larger environment. For instance, perhaps the state library has recently developed a circulating video collection. If your library has selected the role of popular materials library, this may be an opportunity to meet additional community information needs. Identifying activities that take advantage of opportunities are important both in times of growth *and* retrenchment.

When identifying possible activities, you should carefully consider if the activity requires development of a new service and for whom the activity is targeted. These factors should be considered in the context of information from Looking Around (Chapter 3) and Developing Roles and Mission (Chapter 4). There are four broad approaches of user services that may form a basis for identifying activities. The library can develop activities that:

- Increase the frequency with which *current* clientele use *existing* library services
- Expand *new* clientele using *existing* library services
- Encourage *existing* clientele to use *new* library services
- Encourage *new* types of clientele to use *new* types of library services.

Generally, the first two categories require less commitment of effort than the later ones.

Listing Possible Activities

The purpose of this step is to *generate alternative activities,* not to select an activity. One effective approach is to list and briefly describe possible activities for each objective as shown in Workform J, Listing Activities (see Figure 23). This approach encourages participants to focus on activities specifically related to the objectives and to consider alternative activities. Another approach is brainstorming. Some activities may assist a library in achieving two or more objectives. For example, the activity "weeding of the collection" may assist the library in achieving objectives related to increasing turnover rate and to maintaining a more current collection.

Regardless of the approach taken, you should stress suggesting activities that accomplish the stated objectives. Avoid activities that are interesting or appear to be "fun" but which do not support existing roles, goals, and objectives. It is also important to identify at least two possible activities for each objective. Selecting activities for actual implementation does not occur until they are compared and reviewed (see next step).

At a basic level of effort, the library director

Level of Effort for
Taking Action

Basic

   The planning committee or director is largely responsible for identifying possible activities to accomplish each objective and selecting those activities that best accomplish the task. There will be little review and discussion of the activities. The director or another staff member oversees the implementation process by assigning tasks and informally monitoring the staff's progress in accomplishing those tasks. In the middle of this phase, the planning committee completes a short review of the planning *process,* and begins writing the planning document. At the end of this phase, the planning committee reviews the degree to which objectives were, in fact, accomplished. These reviews may take the form of an informal discussion with the director or the director simply reviewing basic factors suggested in this chapter.

Moderate

   The planning committee encourages staff input for identifying and selecting activities. The staff may establish tasks for the activities to help the planning committee compare activities and determine which will best accomplish the objectives. The reviews of the planning *process* and the degree to which objectives were accomplished will be based on written workforms. The director will ensure that tasks for each activity are clearly established and assigned to appropriate staff. The monitoring process will rely on a more formal process such as informal regular reporting or written status reports. The planning committee submits a short written report to the director assessing the status of planning and offering recommendations for the next cycle.

Extensive

   During each step, care is taken to ensure adequate staff participation, input, and review. Brainstorming sessions and/or a workform may be used in the library or in branches to identify activities. Tasks for each activity are detailed prior to selection. Careful comparison based on specific criteria is done to select the best activities. Planning charts are used to ensure effective implementation of the activities. Formal reporting procedures ensure that the director is knowledgeable about the status and effectiveness with which the tasks are being implemented. The planning committee's review of the planning *process* and the degree to which objectives are accomplished are based on staff input. The review is based on criteria in addition to those specified in this chapter, for example, quantitative evidence of the degree to which objectives were accomplished. The report is submitted to the director in writing.

or a member of the planning committee identifies a set of possible activities for each objective. With moderate commitment of effort, the planning committee might have a brainstorming session to identify possible activities. Use of Workform J can assist in this process.

   Librarians wishing to commit a more extensive level of effort can obtain direct input from library staff by asking them to complete and return Workform J (see Figure 23) to the planning committee, hold open "hearings" to identify possible activities, visit neighboring libraries for ideas, and review the professional literature for descriptions of activities used by other libraries.

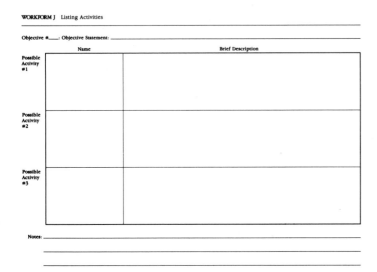

WORKFORM J Listing Activities

Objective #_____: Objective Statement: _____

FIGURE 23   Reduced Workform J: Listing Activities

Result of Identifying Activities

At the completion of this step, a list of possible activities for each objective, from Workform J (see Figure 23), has been identified and briefly described. For example, if the objective is to increase turnover rate from 2.5 to 3.5 during the next year, possible activities might include: weeding the collection, purchasing more best sellers, and opening storefront libraries throughout the community.

Step 3: Select Activities

This step identifies the activity that will *best* accomplish the objective. Having at least two possible activities for each objective encourages creativity and also helps you to *compare* and *contrast* the potential strengths and weaknesses of one activity over another. This comparison forces you to be more realistic, consider potential constraints, and to evaluate the feasibility of each activity.

Listing Tasks

Some librarians may find it useful to list the tasks necessary to accomplish an activity prior to selecting activities. Such a listing is best done by staff due to their knowledge and working experience. The tasks should flow easily from the description of the activity, as shown in Workform J (see Figure 23). The more specific the tasks, the easier the activity can be (1) com-

pared against other activities, (2) implemented, and (3) monitored and evaluated later.

For example, if one possible activity is to weed the collection in an attempt to increase the turnover rate, the tasks (stated at a low level of effort) might be:

- Determine which parts of the collection to weed
- Establish criteria for weeding
- Select staff to weed collection
- Train staff to weed
- Weed collection
- Collect data for turnover rate.

At a basic level of effort there may not be adequate time to develop the tasks for each activity. However, listing tasks is important because it encourages staff to consider the feasibility of the activity. The process also assists in determining *which* activity will *best* accomplish the objective. The tasks listed above for the activity "weeding the collection" are given only as an example. Different and/or additional tasks can be developed depending on level of effort.

Comparing the Activities

Figure 24 describes one approach to compare activities. Criteria included in Figure 24 are suggestive only and not comprehensive. Additional criteria or questions you might ask to assess the activities are:

- Are adequate resources available to implement this activity?
- Which activities best accomplish the objective at the least cost?
- Does the activity capitalize on library strengths and avoid potential weaknesses?
- Will other library services suffer if the activity is implemented?
- Have such activities been used successfully in similar libraries?
- Will implementing the activity call for significant reallocations of library resources?
- Will library staff be committed to the success of the activities, and do they have the necessary competencies to implement them?

Depending on the level of effort for selecting activities, Figure 24 can be used as a basis for discussion or it can be completed in writing. The director and those involved in selecting activities should attempt to select those which have a good chance to succeed. Increased attention to comparing the activities now may increase their success during implementation.

Objective: Increase collection turnover, system-wide, from 2.5 to 3.5 by the end of the current fiscal year.

Criteria	Alternative Activities		
	#1 Weed the Collection	#2 Purchase Best Sellers	#3 Establish Storefront Libraries
1. Staff hours needed to implement the activity	Moderate	Low	High
2. Facilities needed to implement the activity	Few	Some	Many
3. Overall cost of the activity	Low	Moderate	High
4. Feasibility of the activity, i.e., is it doable?	High	Moderate	Low
5. Potential benefits of the activity on the library and the community	Moderate	Moderate	High
6. Degree to which it will help to accomplish the objective	High	Moderate	Low
7. Risk of failure	Low	Low	High
8. Other Criteria (list)			
Activity Rank	First	Second	Third

First preference: Weed the Collection

NOTE: The three alternative activities suggested in this figure are only three of an infinite possible number that might accomplish the stated objective. When assessing the activities on these criteria, different levels of effort can be used—see text for discussion. If desired, quantitative data can be supplied, for example, in no. 3, "Overall cost of the activity," supply figures for estimated costs.

FIGURE 24   Comparing Alternative Activities

Result of Selecting Activities

The planning committee has a list of activities to implement for each objective. If called upon to do so, the director can justify why one activity was selected over another because of the comparison done in Figure 24. These activities, with their corresponding tasks, are now ready for implementation.

Two or more activities for one objective may be identified as feasible and appropriate. The library may choose to implement both. Implementing two activities for a particular objective may increase the likelihood of accomplishing that objective. Ultimately, however, the enthusiasm of the staff and the library's resources will determine how many activities can be selected for implementation.

Step 4: Change the Planning Perspective

At this point in Taking Action, the planning committee should pause to congratulate itself on having completed that part of planning best described as "thinking about what the library will do." Major responsibility for the planning process will now shift to library management and staff for implementing the activities. During this "pause," the planning committee completes two major responsibilities while management and staff proceed with implementation.

Reviewing the Planning Process

The first responsibility of the planning committee during this step is to review the planning *process* thus far. The purpose of the review is to identify those factors that contributed to the success of planning and those factors that can be improved during the next objectives cycle. This review is described in Chapter 8 as Step 3, Reviewing the Planning Process. The planning committee should refer to this section to discuss or complete Workform Q, Summary Workform to Review Planning Process (see Figure 34).

The scope for this review is all of the planning

steps described in Chapter 1 through Chapter 6, Step 3. This review is done only during the first objectives cycle and not in subsequent objectives cycles. At the end of the planning cycle, during Chapter 8, another review of the planning process is done but the context for that review is *the entire* planning cycle.

As suggested in the discussion of Step 3 in Chapter 8, the review can be completed at a very basic level of effort or an extensive level of effort. However, it is important to take time now to conduct this review. The results of the review can be used by the director and the planning committee to improve the effectiveness of the next planning cycle.

Writing the Planning Document

The second responsibility of the planning committee is to oversee the writing of the planning document. Once the activities have been selected, all the information necessary for writing the planning document is available. Generally, library management will want to have a written plan as soon as possible, and now is the time to start writing the plan.

For libraries entering the planning process for the first time, a complete written plan is developed during this step. For libraries in the second or subsequent objectives cycles, the existing planning document is revised and updated.

The planning document can serve a number of different purposes (see Chapter 7). But at this stage of the planning process, what is needed is a document that summarizes the results of planning steps completed thus far. Later in the planning process the planning document can be revised to describe the results of implementation if so desired by the planning committee (see Chapter 8). Thus, the planning committee should now refer to Chapter 7.

The Changed Perspective

The perspective of the planning committee has now changed from directing the planning process to reviewing and summarizing planning steps completed thus far. While the planning committee is reviewing the planning process and writing the plan, library management and staff take responsibility for implementing the plan. In a sense, the "baton" of planning responsibilities has been given to library management and staff. After implementation, the planning committee then completes Step 7, Review Objectives and Activities.

Step 5: Manage Implementation

The director is responsible for this step. Linking the Taking Action process directly to the library's ongoing operations, budget, and staff responsibilities is essential for planning success. Some activities may be scheduled for completion within a budget year. Others, for example, those requiring the library to seek capital development funding or to develop automated services, may require a longer time period.

Charting Time Lines and Implementation Responsibilities

At a moderate and extensive level of effort, a completed chart such as that shown in Figure 25 can assist in implementing and monitoring activities. In small libraries with very few staff, such an approach may not be necessary. But in larger libraries where a number of staff may be working on the activity, this approach can be very useful.

The example shown in Figure 25 is based on the Planning Chart shown in Workform B. It can be used flexibly and may be modified during implementation if the need arises. The greater the effort given to completing Workform B, the greater the likelihood that the activity will be successful and easy to monitor later (see next step). If the tasks do not appear to be feasible, or are difficult to assign to staff or to schedule, the activity needs to be revised.

The director may assign some tasks to an individual and others to a group. However, activities that are the responsibility of one person may be easier to monitor than those assigned to a group. Both approaches can be used successfully to accomplish objectives. But, matching staff competencies to the tasks is a key factor for the overall success of Taking Action.

Ensuring Measurement Data

Some objectives may require baseline data before implementation of the activity. Take, for example, the objective "increase title fill rate by 15% during the current fiscal year." The library needs to know the existing title fill rate. Unless the library already has such data, the first task for the activity, then, is to collect that baseline data.

Usually one of the tasks for each activity is to obtain measurement data either during or at the end of the activity. *OMPL,* second edition, provides procedures for collecting a number of output measures and offers suggestions for developing others. It is important to remember to

Activity Name: Weeding Collection

Task	Person	Month 1	2	3	4	5	6	7	8	9	10	11	12
1. Determine collection parts to weed.	A	X											
2. Establish criteria for weeding.	A	X											
3. Develop schedule for who is to weed which part and when.	B		X										
4. Train staff on how to weed.	B plus staff		X										
5. Develop tracking log for each day's weeding.	A		X										
6. Establish measures to assess effectiveness and efficiency.	A			X									
7. Determine disposition of weeded material.	A and B			X									
8. Begin weeding process.	Staff			X									
9. Complete tracking log on daily basis.	B			X	X	X	X	X	X	X			
10. Monitor and evaluate process.	A					X			X				
11. Complete weeding process.	Staff										X		
12. Collect data for title fill rate.	A											X	

Notes and Explanations: For this particular activity, no additional significant resources are necessary.

FIGURE 25 Example Planning Chart

include the task of collecting data to measure the success of the objective (see, for example, task #12 in Figure 25).

Results of Managing Implementation

At the completion of this step, staff should know who is responsible for accomplishing what tasks by when. A planning chart such as that shown in Figure 25 can assist in this process. The detail included in the chart depends on the level of effort committed by the library. The director now makes staff assignments and allocates resources to implement the tasks. The library staff is now actively involved in completing tasks.

Staff are now implementing the activities and completing the tasks. The process of implementation and completing tasks will take a number of months and perhaps as long as two years. Monitoring should be done throughout this entire period.

Step 6: Monitor the Implementation Process

Monitoring is essential. Library managers cannot assume that because responsibilities have been assigned and resources made available, that tasks, in fact, are done. A completed chart, such as that shown in Figure 25, is an excellent means to monitor the implementation of the tasks.

At higher levels of effort, Workform K, Activities Status Report (see Figure 26), provides a more formal means for staff to regularly report the status of the implementation process. The director, or person responsible for the activity, can circulate this form to staff on a regular basis, for example, every three months. Increased attention to monitoring is likely to increase the success with which the activities are implemented.

Monitoring the implementation process from many perspectives helps produce the "big picture" of how activities are affecting each other as well as the library's overall service patterns. Thus, effective monitoring of the implementation process may require reporting by a number of different individuals or units in the library.

Based on the information obtained during the monitoring process, library managers should provide feedback and suggestions to those implementing the activities. If changes in the tasks, responsibilities, or time lines are needed, they

WORKFORM K   Activities Status Report

Person Reporting: _____ Date: _____

Objective: _____

Activity Name: _____

Tasks: (If available, append completed Planning Charts, Workform B).

Current Status on implementing tasks:

1. Are the tasks being implemented on schedule?

2. Are adequate resources/equipment available?

3. Have any problems been encountered with implementing the tasks?

4. Are revisions needed for the tasks or for the planning chart? If yes, please detail:

Comments/Suggestions from Director or Planning Committee:

NOTE: To be used for moderate or extensive level of effort only.

FIGURE 26   Reduced Workform K: Activities Status Report

can be made during implementation. Do not wait until the end of implementation to discover that changes should have been made months ago!

If the implementation of an activity is laden with difficulties, it may be necessary to reassess the appropriateness of this particular activity. You may wish to use a different activity to accomplish the objective. Again, now is the time to make that decision rather than allowing the implementation process to continue to falter.

Step 7: Review Objectives and Activities

This is the last step of Taking Action and occurs at the end of each objectives cycle. The planning committee conducts this review and identifies factors that contributed to the success or failure of *accomplishing objectives and implementing activities.* Note that this review has a different focus than that done in Step 4. Step 4 reviews the planning *process;* this step reviews the planning *results.* Based on the review of objectives and activities, the planning committee and staff can learn from their experiences so that the next objectives cycle can be improved.

Information for the Review

Workform L, Assessment of Activities and Objectives (see Figure 27), provides an outline of information necessary to complete the review of objectives and activities. During the review, librarians may identify additional information needed to develop new objectives for the next cycle. For example, staff may decide that additional information is needed to describe the age of materials in the nonfiction area before they decide on the appropriateness of new objectives related to weeding.

It is important to consider the results of output measures (or other types of measures) when reviewing the overall success of accomplishing an objective. Item "E" of Workform L provides space to report this information. When reviewing the output measures also consider the factors that may have affected the results. *OMPL,* second edition, discusses a number of possible factors that may affect library performance on individual output measures.

Depending on the information required or changes in community or library conditions, the planning committee may choose to insert a supplemental Looking Around process prior to setting new objectives. The key point, however, is that the library director or planning committee review the implementation of activities and the degree to which objectives were accomplished.

WORKFORM L Assessment of Activities and Objectives

A. Objective # :

B. Activity(ies) used to accomplish this objective:

C. Strengths and weaknesses of the activity(ies):

D. Recommendations to improve these activities:

E. Evidence of the degree to which the objective was accomplished:

F. Factors that contributed to or hindered the accomplishment of the objectives:

G. Additional information needed from a "Supplemental Looking Around" regarding this objective prior to the next objectives cycle.

H. Recommendations for this objective for the next objectives cycle:

FIGURE 27 Reduced Workform L: Assessment of Activities and Objectives

Result of Reviewing Objectives and Activities

The result of this step of Taking Action is an assessment that includes two basic parts. The first assesses the results of the activities, assesses the appropriateness of each objective during that objectives cycle, and offers recommendations for objectives and activities during the next objectives cycle (or planning cycle). This portion is based largely on information provided in Workform L (see Figure 27).

The second portion summarizes information collected as a result of Step 4, when the planning committee reviewed the planning process. The content of this portion of the report is based largely on information obtained from Workform Q, Summary Workform to Review Planning Process. The planning committee produces this summary for the director, who reviews it and can make changes to improve the next objectives cycle.

At a basic level of effort, you may not need to conduct this review in writing. It can be an informal discussion of the factors identified in Workforms L and Q. At a moderate level of effort, the report is more formal and does rely on completing Workforms L and Q in writing. The planning committee may wish to have a number of discussions about the information contained on these workforms before submitting the report to the director.

Planning committees conducting the review at an extensive level of effort will want not only to complete Workforms L and Q, they will also want to:

• Include more quantitative summary information, such as budget information, staff costs, output measure data, and so forth
• Obtain information other than that suggested from Workforms L and Q
• Allow for additional staff involvement and discussion in the review process.

The greater the attention given to conducting this review, the greater the likelihood that library staff can learn from their planning experiences and improve the next objectives or planning cycle.

Sources for Additional Information

Kotler, Phillip. *Marketing for Non-Profit Organizations.* Englewood Cliffs, N.J.: Prentice-Hall, 1985.

The discussion of categories of user services, on pages 166–167, may be useful in identifying possible activities.

Riggs, Donald E. *Strategic Planning for Library Managers.* Phoenix, Ariz.: Oryx Press, 1984.

Examples of additional types of planning and implementation charts are provided in this source on pages 104–108.

Van House, Nancy A., Mary Jo Lynch, Charles R. McClure, Douglas Zweizig, and Eleanor Jo Rodger. *Output Measures for Public Libraries.* Second edition. Chicago: American Library Association, 1987.

When tasking activities, reference to this source can provide an idea of the amount of time and resources that might be required for ensuring the availability of measurement data.

Writing the Planning Document

One important product of the planning process is a planning document. It formalizes the work done during planning, informs the public of the results of planning, and serves as a reference source for future library decision making. The planning document describes the planning activities that have occurred and might also describe those expected to occur in the remainder of the planning cycle.

The two most important aims in writing the planning document are that it is an accurate representation of the library's planning and that it communicates this information effectively to the library's board, community, and local government officials.

This chapter offers guidelines for the development of a written planning document. Three possible versions of a planning document will be outlined, based on three different levels of effort. The basic steps include:

1. Prepare to write the planning document
2. Determine the level of effort
3. Write the planning document
4. Review the planning document
5. Obtain formal approval for the planning document
6. Present and promote the planning document.

The result of these steps is a completed, written planning document that has been approved by appropriate library governing bodies and disseminated to community groups, agencies, and other interested individuals.

Step 1: Prepare to Write the Planning Document

Attention to a few factors before writing the planning document can save much time and ef-

fort. In fact, much of the work has already been done. Remaining activities are largely organizing existing planning information, reworking that information for public dissemination, and ensuring that the planning document represents the correct "image" of the library.

Planning Document Time Frame

The planning committee has a number of options for when to produce the planning document. It may be written after:

- Goals and objectives are stated (end of Chapter 5)
- Activities have been decided upon but before they are implemented (middle of Chapter 6)
- Reviewing the objectives and activities (end of Chapter 6).

The discussion in Step 4 of Chapter 6 recommends the second option: after activities have been determined. But, depending on individual situations, local government requirements, the desires of the director, or other factors, some libraries may produce a planning document at other points in the planning process.

At the completion of each objectives cycle (typically every year), the planning document should be updated and revised (or an addendum attached) to reflect any changes. Some libraries have found that keeping the planning document in a loose-leaf notebook simplifies revisions and updating. But the portion of the planning document describing roles, mission statement, and goals is not likely to change during a planning cycle. The start of a new planning cycle signals the need for another planning document.

Administrative Organization

It is often best for the planning committee or the library director to appoint one individual to be responsible for drafting the planning document. The writer produces a draft which is reviewed and revised, and then prepares the final version. Some desirable characteristics for the person writing the draft include:

- Previous involvement with the planning process and membership on the planning committee
- Writing skills and experience
- Ability to consider/accept comments and suggestions from others when the document is revised and edited.

Other library staff members may contribute to drafting parts of the planning document. Generally, the person responsible for writing the document will know if additional assistance is necessary and who might be able and willing to contribute. If others contribute to the writing, they should receive clear guidelines describing their responsibilities.

Depending on the level of effort committed to the planning document, clerical support for typing or word processing the document, graphics design, copying, and collation/binding of the document may require significant staff time. The director should provide adequate resources to support these activities.

Organizing Existing Planning Information

Much of the information for the planning document was produced in earlier phases of the planning process. Key sources to use as input for writing the planning document include:

- Planning Responsibilities (Step 3, Chapter 2)
- Budget for Planning (Workform A)
- Planning Chart (Workform B)
- Options for Library Planning Information (Workform C)
- Translating the Findings of Looking Around (Workform D)
- Report of the Results of Looking Around (Step 6, Chapter 3)
- Output Measure Results (Chapter 3 and Chapter 6)
- Summary of Roles, Goals, and Objectives (Workform I)
- Planning Charts [for each activity] (as per example in Figure 25)
- Assessment of Activities and Objectives (Workform L).

These and possibly other items should be gathered and made available to the individual responsible for drafting the planning document.

Other Issues

Before writing, the planning committee should decide on the following issues:

- *Who are the primary audiences for the planning document?* Is it the library staff, the library board, local government officials, library clientele, or the general public? Determining the intended target audiences first allows those writing the document to focus the content and complexity to that particular target audience.

• *How will the planning document be designed and formatted?* Will the document be a typed report or will it include sophisticated graphics and be typeset? Graphics and other design factors enhance the attractiveness of the document but also add to the time required and the cost.

• *How much staff time can be committed to writing the planning document?* Any publication for external distribution can be revised and edited endlessly, if such is allowed to occur. A clear deadline date for the production of the planning document and the level of commitment for its production should be made before the writing begins.

These three issues may be independent of the levels of effort suggested in the following sections. A planning document based on a low level of effort but incorporating substantial design and graphics may require the same level of library resources (but different types) as a planning document following the guidelines for a high level of effort.

Step 2: Determine Level of Effort

The planning committee should consider factors presented in Figure 28 before writing the document. More experienced writers may wish to "mix and match" the levels of effort on each factor. For example, one library might spend a low level of effort on overall length of the document but spend a high level of effort on graphics.

The Level of Effort Box for Writing the Planning Document and Figure 29 provide additional discussion regarding options for developing the planning document. Generally, libraries committing higher levels of effort to writing the planning document do so for any of the following reasons:

• The production/review of the planning document is structured in such a way that library staff participate in the process as a learning experience

• The planning document is a key internal document that will guide library decision making in the foreseeable future and will be referred to frequently

• The planning document is used as a key item for distribution to government officials, community leaders, or other individuals to increase the visibility of the library within the community.

Although the length of the planning document increases considerably from a low to high level of effort, the conciseness, crispness, and clear organization/presentation of information should be the same across all levels of effort. Length, in itself, will not necessarily improve the document!

Step 3: Write the Planning Document

At this point, the person responsible for drafting the planning document begins to write. That

Level of Effort	Time Commitment	Length of Document	Use of Graphics	Purposes of Content
Basic	1—2 Working Days 1 Person	7—12 Pages	None or Limited	Describe*
Moderate	5—10 Working Days 1—2 People	15—30 Pages	Moderate Hand-made	Describe* Explain**
High	More Than 10 Working Days More Than 3 People	40 Pages or More	Frequent Microcomputer generated or produced by a graphic designer	Describe* Explain** Analyze***

   *Describe: report the planning events that occurred and the products from those events
  **Explain: discuss the process that produced the planning events and the factors affecting that process
***Analyze: explain *why* the planning events and results occurred as they did and interpret their meaning and implications for library decision making

FIGURE 28 Factors Affecting Level of Effort for Writing the Planning Document

Level of Effort for
Writing the Planning Document

Basic

At a basic level of effort, one person, often the director, takes responsibility for producing a draft of the planning document, which should be produced within one or two working days. The person first collects the information for sections C–F (see Figure 29). After these sections have been organized and edited, the person writes the introduction and summary. Writing the executive summary last takes less time since the writer can simply review the information in other sections of the draft and "pull out" the key points that need to be stressed. The document may be reviewed by members of the planning committee, key staff members, or perhaps the library board.

Moderate

The length of the document as well as the detail of information provided increases at this level of effort. Additional staff may assist in drafting certain sections of the document. New sections are included (see Figure 29). Sections describing the results of Looking Around and the Selection of Roles will be more detailed and may be presented with graphics. Further, the discussions of the roles, mission statement, goals and objectives should also briefly *explain* the process by which they were developed.

The person responsible for drafting the planning document spends 5–10 person-days on its development. Additional attention, at this level of effort, will be given to the use of graphics, subheadings, and selecting *only* that information resulting from the planning process that may be of interest to one or two target audiences. The review would include selected library staff, members of the planning committee, or library board.

Extensive

Figure 29 provides guidelines for the types of information that might be contained in a planning document at this level of effort. In addition to the new sections, the primary difference between this level of effort and that at a moderate level is the extent of the *analysis,* that is, what do the data mean? How are they related to library services? To what degree can the library respond to identified needs in the next objectives setting cycle? At this level of effort, greater introspection, analysis of implications from the planning process, and "pulling out" of recommendations and changes for the next objectives review cycle are needed.

In addition to changes in the content, length, and purposes of the planning document, more attention is given to graphics, targeting information to specific audiences, and typesetting/design of the plan. Overall attractiveness of the planning document should be an important consideration at this level of effort. The review process will be more extensive, including additional individuals from the library, planning committee, board, community, and perhaps local government officials. Further, the writer may produce different executive summaries for specific target audiences.

person should keep in mind the decisions made in Steps 1 and 2. Figure 29 offers guidelines for the organization and content of the planning document. But regardless of the level of effort committed to writing the document, the planning document should be:

- Well-organized and include frequent section headings and subheadings
- Jargon free—avoid terms with special meanings for librarians if the intended audience is nonlibrarians
- Attractive in appearance—pages should not look "cluttered"; include adequate "white space" on each page
- Visually oriented—avoid continuous pages of text; when appropriate, include summary graphics, tables, and figures which are individually labeled for easy reference from any point in the text.

Throughout, strive for a clear, crisp, and concise writing style that gets directly at the point.

Remember that, generally, the planning document is a *summary* document intended for public dissemination. If the planning committee wants a detailed history of how a library planned, a second more extensive planning document for internal use can also be produced.

Step 4: Review the Planning Document

Do not expect the planning document draft to be "perfect." Reviewing it is important because the process:

- Allows others associated with the planning process to provide input and, thus, to increase their sense of "ownership" of the document
- Obtains other viewpoints about the content and organization of the document before its dissemination as a public document
- Educates those reviewing the planning document about the planning process in the library
- Assists in editing and generally increases the accuracy and readability of the document.

Depending on the level of effort, the review of the draft planning document may occur from both within and outside the library. Within the library, obtain input from the planning committee or key library staff regarding the content and organization of the document. From outside the library, obtain input from the library board. Further, someone from the community, not associated with the planning process, might review the document for readability, clarity, and overall interest.

The director should review the document within the political context of the local community. The acknowledgements section might recognize the contributions and interest of key elected officials. Or perhaps, it might make good political sense not to discuss past library services that caused considerable controversy.

During the review process, focus *both* on content and organization of material as well as wording, style, and grammar. The last three items are easier to critique than content and organization. Ultimately, the persons writing the document will incorporate their own writing style. As a general rule, reviewers should have at least one opportunity, but probably no more than two, to review the draft before it is finalized. Do not allow the *process* of reviewing the document to replace its *completion*.

Reviews can be done by holding formal meetings to discuss the document. Or, they can be done by distributing copies of the draft and asking the planning committee members, community target groups, or staff to "mark it up" with suggestions and comments. Once the suggestions have been obtained, the person(s) responsible for writing the draft produce a final version which is then submitted to the director for approval.

Step 5: Obtain Formal Approval for the Planning Document

Public libraries in the United States report to a range of different agencies or organizational bodies. Many have boards which are legally responsible for all library activities; in others, the board serves only in an advisory capacity. In some cases, the director may report directly to a local governmental official and may not have a library board.

Where there is a governing body, the director will want it to approve the document. Where the board is advisory, it should formally endorse the planning document. Obtaining formal approval/endorsement of the planning document:

- Increases the board's knowledge regarding library operations and services
- Encourages consensus among the board members and director about library priorities
- Provides direct and visible evidence that the board supports the activities and services of the library

Document Section	Level of Effort		
	Basic	Moderate	Extensive
Front Matter	Provide a well-organized, easy-to-read title page, Acknowledgements, and a Table of Contents.	Same as basic level of effort.	Same as basic level of effort.
A. Executive Summary	Include a brief overview of the entire planning document and summarize roles, mission statement, goals, and objectives.	Same as basic level of effort, but 2—3 pages.	Same as moderate level of effort except that it includes a summary of the recommendations from Section J below.
B. Introduction	Importance and need for planning and explain the library's structure for roles, goals, and objectives.	Same as basic level of effort but also describe the process by which planning was done in the library.	Same as moderate level of effort.
C. Basic Information about the Library	Exclude	Describe existing library priorities and activities, the physical facility, and recent budget information. Include an organization chart and a map depicting the location of the library and its branches.	Same as moderate level but add a final section that analyzes the availability of critical resources and the performance of the library on selected measures. Present an analysis of the impact of library conditions on services, their effect on clientele, and possible future factors that may affect these conditions.
D. Community Conditions and Clientele/ Library Needs	Summary of information from Looking Around (Chapter 3).	The summary should be more detailed than that presented at the basic level. Include an explanation of the process by which the information was collected. Include summary graphics from Chapter 3 about (1) internal conditions, (2) external conditions, and (3) community information needs.	Same as moderate level but add detailed information from Looking Around with discussion of the reliability and validity of the data. Add a discussion that analyzes the impact of library conditions on services, specific needs of the clientele, and how the library might respond to those needs.
E. Overview of Needs	Exclude	Exclude	Provide a summary of library and community needs based on sections C and D.
F. Roles and Mission Statement	List the library roles and level of commitment to each. Include a copy of the mission statement.	List roles and mission statement with a brief justification and description of the process by which they were developed.	List roles and mission statement and explain the process by which they were developed. Analyze community conditions, critical resources, and output measures to justify the roles and mission.

FIGURE 29 Planning Document Guidelines

- Informs the local community of library priorities and activities during the planning cycle
- Establishes a formal "document of reference," i.e., the document can be referred to again at a later date to verify and justify decisions
- Allows the library to, at a later date, return to the board and demonstrate the degree to which the intended objectives were accomplished.

Document Section	Level of Effort		
	Basic	Moderate	Extensive
G. Goals and Objectives	Include a copy of the goals and objectives.	List the goals, objectives, and measures for each objective. Explain briefly the process by which they were developed.	Same as moderate level but justify the objectives in terms of library and community conditions. Measures for each of the objectives are listed and justified.
H. Activities	Exclude	List the activities that were established for each of the objectives.	List the activities for each of the objectives, estimate and justify the costs for implementing them.
I. Summary and Anticipated Planning Activities	A one—two-page reinforcement of key points in the plan with a list of activities to occur the next year.	Same as basic level of effort but provide greater detail.	Same as moderate level but list specific benefits and tangible results from the planning process.
FOR ANNUAL UPDATE ONLY J. Review of Previous Year's Objectives	Provide a brief statement of the degree to which the objectives were accomplished.	Same as basic level of effort.	In addition to the moderate level, explain and analyze the degree to which they were accomplished (if available).
FOR ANNUAL UPDATE ONLY K. Recommendations for the Next Objectives Cycle	Exclude	Brief overview of areas where changes should occur.	Offer specific recommendations for the next objectives cycle, e.g., critical resources needed, measures to assess objectives, or possible activities.
L. Appendixes	Exclude	Include here copies of data collection instruments, data summaries too lengthy for inclusion in the text, or other planning useful information.	Same as moderate level.

FIGURE 29   Planning Document Guidelines (continued)

The planning document is an important means for the library to obtain increased visibility from the community and establish greater credibility for its programs and activities.

The process for obtaining formal approval may vary depending on the organizational/administrative structure under which the library works. If the library has a library board that is responsible for policy decisions, a typical procedure would be to:

• Include at least one or two board members in the initial review of the draft planning document

• Distribute the final planning document to board members well in advance of the board meeting at which it will be discussed

• Make a presentation to the board summarizing the document and highlighting important aspects of the planning document (see suggestions in the following section)

• Discuss the document with the board, answer questions, and listen to suggestions or comments

• Have a member of the board move for approval of the planning document if the response from the board is positive. If concerns are raised about the document, it may be necessary to make some revisions and schedule a meeting to approve the document at a later date.

During this process, the director should work closely with the chairperson of the board in organizing the meetings, discussing the key aspects of the planning document, and allowing adequate time for review and comments.

After the planning document is approved, an adequate number of copies should be made and distributed. Determine who should obtain copies and estimate how many additional copies are needed for promoting the library's planning process.

Step 6: Present and Promote the Planning Document

Now that the planning document has been written, distribute it to appropriate people such as government officials, community leaders, the state librarian, and other librarians. But simply distributing the planning document to such people may not have the same impact as a *presentation* of the document to them. Such presentations will increase the visibility of the library and inform the larger community about the planning document.

Consider the following factors when developing an oral presentation to promote the planning document:

• Who is the audience for the presentation and what is its current level of understanding regarding the library or library planning? Organize and present the planning information accordingly.
• How much time is available for the presentation? Do not annoy the audience by exceeding the time allotted.
• What image do you want the library to project— maintaining the status quo in light of cutbacks? leading the community into a new information age? or offering new and improved services for children?
• What, specifically, are the key points that you wish to stress to this particular audience?
• Will there be adequate time for you to answer questions or to meet later, informally, with members of the audience?
• Will you be able to use visuals and/or handouts during the presentation? Generally, the

use of slides, overhead transparencies, and summary handouts enhance a presentation.

In such presentations, use notes or, better, use handouts and visuals to serve as "notes" while talking informally. Also keep in mind that audiences are most typically interested in the impact of the planning process on *them*. Thus, the presenter should identify specific aspects of the planning document and areas where changes might occur that affect that audience. Discuss these items in greater detail.

Some libraries produce a planning document summary of a few pages for distribution to special target audiences. Additional coverage can be obtained from news releases and interviews by local newspapers with the library director and/or planning committee.

Depending on the resources and level of commitment, a significant effort might be committed to promoting the planning document throughout the library's community. Getting *out of the library* to make presentations is an important means of shaping the image of the library and promoting its overall effectiveness. Thus, the (1) content and the format of the planning document, and (2) the manner in which it is presented and promoted will convey an image of the library. The library director should carefully consider what image to project and work toward fulfilling that image.

Sources for Additional Information

Edsall, Marian S. *Library Promotion Handbook*. Phoenix, Ariz.: Oryx Press, 1980.
    This is a very practical approach for promoting the library, and a number of the chapters contain useful information for writing materials and making presentations.
Zinsser, William. *On Writing Well*. Third edition. New York: Harper & Row, 1985.
    This book is a basic style manual. It offers excellent practical suggestions related to style, grammar, and writing clearly.

Reviewing Results

8

Results are reviewed at several points during the planning cycle. In the Taking Action phase of the first objectives cycle, the planning committee reviews the results of planning after the selection of objectives and activities (see Chapter 6, Step 4). At the end of each objectives cycle, the planning committee identifies the factors that led to the success or failure of accomplishing objectives and implementing activities (Chapter 6, Step 7). Finally, at the end of each planning cycle (3–5 years), the entire planning process is reviewed as described in this chapter. These reviews should be seen as preparation for future planning activities. Thus, they should be as brief as possible and be seen as a *means* to the larger ends of improving overall library planning.

As a result of completing the phases described earlier in this manual, those involved in planning will have gained a substantial amount of experience. Since planning is an ongoing process, it is important to learn from that experience and to use this knowledge in the next planning cycle. Reviewing Results helps each planning cycle increase in effectiveness and usefulness.

Overall, Reviewing Results focuses on three broad areas:

• The *plan:* Were objectives accomplished? To what degree are the goals, mission statement, and roles appropriate? What impacts did planning have on library services overall? To what degree were the information needs of the library's clientele better met?

• The *planning process:* Were group meetings effective? Was there too little or too much data collection? Were library staff adequately trained to participate in the planning process? Were

the selected level of efforts for portions of the planning process appropriate?

- *Recycling:* How can the library staff profit from their planning experiences in the next planning cycle? What specific "lessons" should be integrated into the next Planning to Plan phase?

The purpose of the review is to make a set of recommendations which can be used by the director and planning committee to improve the decisions for the next planning cycle.

This chapter suggests a way to identify areas where library planning can be improved for the next cycle. It includes four basic steps:

1. Determine level of effort
2. Review the plan
3. Review the planning process
4. Recycle the information.

In preparation for the review, the review of the planning process done in the first objectives cycle (Step 4, Chapter 6), the annual review of objectives and activities (Step 7, Chapter 6), the annual planning documents (as described in Chapter 7), and planning information from other planning phases should be collected to assist with the review. Make certain that those individuals conducting the review have easy access to this material.

Step 1: Determine Level of Effort

Both the review and recycling processes are important to the overall, ongoing success of library planning. The review can be organized in different ways:

- Director and/or top library administration conduct the review
- Planning committee conducts the review
- The director appoints either a subcommittee of the planning committee or a separate committee responsible for conducting the review.

Generally, the more people involved in the review the greater are the level of effort and the amount of time and resources necessary.

Librarians who commit an extensive level of effort to the review process may do so for a number of reasons. The director may wish to make certain that the next planning cycle is significantly improved, a number of concerns may have been identified throughout the planning process that require attention, or library staff might be very interested in the planning/evaluation process and the director wishes to encourage continued interest.

On the other hand, the review may be completed at a basic level of effort based primarily on informal discussions among key library staff. A basic level of effort may be adequate if no significant problems occurred with the planning process; the director, planning committee, and staff are generally satisfied with both the planning process and the plan; or if there are simply other more important priorities for the library to address. The critical concern, however, is that a review does, in fact, occur—regardless of the level of effort.

Step 2: Review the Plan

The broad purpose of this review is to determine the degree to which the plan improved overall library performance. Areas for review are, first, results from Taking Action, next, the objectives, goals, mission statement, and roles, and last, the information gathered from Looking Around. The review determines the appropriateness and usefulness of these items. Depending on the level of effort committed to reviewing the results of planning, you may wish to modify or use some or all of the workforms in this chapter.

Activities and Objectives

Much of the review of activities and objectives has already been done in each objectives cycle and recorded on Workform L. These workforms should be collected and referred to during this step. In addition, reviewers may wish to assess:

- To what degree were the levels of effort actually required to implement the activities consistent with the levels originally chosen?
- Was the level of effort worth the results? Why?
- How did the objectives support the library's roles, mission, and goals?
- To what degree did the objectives assist in generating ideas for activities?
- Were the objectives modified and refined on a regular basis during the planning cycle?
- Were adequate resources available to accomplish the objectives? If not, why not?

It is important to review *all* the objectives and activities agreed upon during the planning cycle to obtain the "big picture."

Goals

Review the goals next. The following questions can serve as discussion points:

- To what degree did the goal contribute toward the overall mission of the library (or branch)?

Level of Effort for
Reviewing Results

Basic

   The director, a member of the planning committee, or staff informally reviews previously completed Workform L (Figure 27) to assess the planning process. Workforms M, N, O, and P (Figures 30–33) guide the review of the plan. If time is limited for the review, the reviewer should concentrate on considering those parts of the workforms that ask for recommendations to improve the next planning cycle. The director may obtain some input from staff. The entire review may be completed informally but it is recommended that Workform R (Figure 35) is completed in writing. The director ensures that these recommendations are considered by the next planning committee for the next planning cycle.

Moderate

   The planning committee or a specially established committee reviews Workform L (Figure 27) after the first objectives cycle, and completes Workforms M, N, O, P, Q, and R (Figures 30–35). This process can be done in meetings or by establishing task forces to review specific aspects of the plan or the planning process. One member of the review committee could develop a first draft of the completed workforms for discussion by the planning committee. After discussion, the director or planning committee produces final recommendations. If possible, members of the next planning committee are involved in the review. The director develops appropriate techniques to integrate these recommendations into the development of the next planning cycle.

Extensive

   Members of the library staff become directly involved in the review. One approach is to have staff members serve on various task forces. Another approach is to have library staff participate in "open hearings" on specific aspects of the planning process or the plan. Further, questionnaires can be distributed to staff to obtain input on all or some of the factors listed in the workforms presented throughout this chapter.
   The planning committee may wish to expand the criteria shown on the various workforms and topics presented in this chapter when assessing the planning process and the plan. Additional questions to be considered are included throughout the chapter. A more detailed set of recommendations are written based on Workform R (Figure 35) and other criteria. The director may wish to meet with the planning committee to discuss the recommendations in greater detail. The recommendations are recycled into the next planning committee by group discussions, "open hearings," a presentation by the director, or direct involvement from previous members of the planning committee.

• To what degree did the goal assist in fulfilling one or more of the agreed upon roles?
• Were the goals mutually supportive or were there instances in which the goals competed with one another?
• How well did the goals assist library staff in developing objectives?

Workform M, Review of Goals (see Figure 30), summarizes the review of goals and assists in developing recommendations for revising goals.

Roles and Mission Statement

Workform N, Review of Roles (see Figure 31), can assist in the review of roles and mission. In addition, consider the degree to which:

• Library staff were able to base the goals and objectives on the roles and mission
• Library services during the planning cycle changed or resources were redirected to support a particular role
• Primary and secondary roles were appropriate.

WORKFORM M Review of Goals

Goal Statement: _____

A. How did this goal assist in fulfilling the library's mission?

_____

_____

B. To what degree did this goal enable the library to fulfill its roles? Which roles, specifically, does this goal address?

_____

_____

C. How did this goal support or compete with other goals?

_____

_____

D. To what extent did this goal provide a basis from which library staff could write clear and measurable objectives?

_____

_____

_____

E .Recommendations for revising this goal statement:
   [ ] maintain the goal as currently written
   [ ] drop this goal
   [ ] revise this goal in the following manner: _____

_____

_____

_____

FIGURE 30 Reduced Workform M: Review of Goals

WORKFORM N Review of Roles

Role Name: _____ Level of Commitment: _____

A. Adequacy of critical resources to fulfill this role:

_____

_____

_____

B. Indicators of fulfilling this role (include appropriate output measures):

_____

_____

_____

C. Changes in library or community conditions that affected or may affect this role:

_____

_____

_____

D. Recommendations for changing the role or its level of commitment:

_____

_____

_____

FIGURE 31 Reduced Workform N: Review of Roles

Examine the mission statement next. This review is based, in part, on the review of the roles and the reviewers' perceptions of significant changes that occurred in the library or the community since the previous planning cycle. Recommendations from the reviews of activities, objectives, goals, and roles should be considered as well as an intuitive "feel" for the li-brary's mission. Workform O, Review of Mission Statement (see Figure 32), summarizes the review of the mission statement.

Results of Looking Around

Depending on the level of effort committed to Looking Around (Chapter 3), summary reports were produced as a basis for selecting roles and stating goals and objectives. The reviewers should assess the usefulness of the information in the reports, now that the planning cycle has been completed.

Consider also the recommendations from Workform L regarding supplementary Looking Arounds and determine if there are implications for data collection and analysis. You also may wish to assess other criteria such as the reliability of the data and the degree to which the information was actually used in developing roles, goals, and objectives. Workform P, Review of Information Gathered by Looking Around (see Figure 33), provides a summary for the review of Looking Around information. The more specific these recommendations are, the easier it will be to improve the next Looking Around.

Step 3: Review the Planning Process

Some of you will be completing this step as part of Step 4 of Chapter 6; others will be completing it as part of the sequence in Chapter 8. The level of effort committed to this step if done as part of the review of the entire planning cycle may depend on the effort dedicated to it earlier in Step 4 of Chapter 6.

For example, if the planning committee is very satisfied with the review that occurred as a result of Step 4 of Chapter 6, it may be necessary to conduct only a brief review now. If, on the other hand, significant changes and problems occurred with the planning process after that review, additional effort probably should be given to this final review.

Regardless of the level of effort committed to answering such questions and conducting this review, you can select from the following topics or issues those that seem to be especially important for your particular library: budget, staff time, planning participants' roles, the planning schedule, appropriateness of the levels of effort, communication, and other factors.

Two basic approaches can be used to obtain information for this review: (1) library reports and other in-house materials, and (2) discussions with or surveys of participants in the planning process. Workform Q, Summary Workform to Review Planning Cycle (see Figure 34), can be used to focus a discussion and/or record the findings of the review as it proceeds through the following topics.

Review of Library Records

BUDGET

Begin by reviewing the planning budget developed during Planning to Plan (Chapter 2). At the end of the planning cycle, the total costs for the planning process can be computed and compared, category by category, to the original estimates. Based on these comparisons, the following questions can be asked:

• What planning costs were more or less than expected? Why?
• What costs were incurred that were not budgeted? Do these costs need to be included in the next planning budget?
• Overall, were planning costs acceptable and worthwhile? If not, why not?

STAFF TIME

The use of staff time in the planning process may be a critical factor affecting the success of planning. Thus, it is important to consider the topic separately. Basic questions to ask here are:

• Were the estimates of staff's time to be involved in the planning process accurate? If not, why not?
• How did staff involvement in the planning process affect other library services and operations?
• In which planning steps is additional staff time necessary and in which can staff time be reduced?
• Could volunteers or other nonlibrary staff members successfully assist in the planning process? In which steps?

PLANNING PARTICIPANTS' ROLES

Throughout the planning process, a number of different individuals and groups may have participated in the process. A review of their activities can consider:

• To what degree were planning participants' responsibilities clearly defined, or revised and clarified as needed throughout the planning process? Why or in what ways?
• Are changes needed in the responsibilities for these individuals or groups for the next planning cycle? What, specifically, are these changes?

FIGURE 32 Reduced Workform O: Review of Mission Statement

FIGURE 33 Reduced Workform P: Review of Information Gathered by Looking Around

WORKFORM Q Summary Workform to Review Planning Process

A. Review of Library Records

1. Budget

Summary Comments: _____

_____

_____

Recommendations: _____

_____

_____

_____

2. Staff Time

Summary Comments: _____

_____

Recommendations: _____

_____

_____

3. Planning Participants' Roles

Summary Comments: _____

_____

Recommendations: _____

_____

_____

4. The Planning Schedule

Summary Comments: _____

_____

Recommendations: _____

_____

_____

5. Levels of Effort

Summary Comments: _____

_____

Recommendations: _____

_____

_____

6. Internal Communication

Summary Comments: _____

_____

Recommendations: _____

_____

_____

7. Other Factors

Summary Comments: _____

_____

Recommendations: _____

_____

_____

B. Discussions and Surveys

Summary Comments: _____

_____

_____

Recommendations: _____

_____

_____

FIGURE 34   Reduced Workform Q: Summary Workform to Review Planning Process

• How could administrative lines of authority among the various planning participants be made clearer and be better understood?
• If problems or issues arose during the planning process, were they resolved by the appropriate individuals? If not, why not?
• To what degree were the right people involved in the planning process at the right time?

THE PLANNING SCHEDULE

At several points in the planning process (Planning to Plan, Looking Around, Writing Goals and Objectives, and Taking Action) planning charts may have been developed. A review of these planning charts should consider:

• To what degree were tasks adequately defined and detailed?
• Was the sequencing of the tasks appropriate? If not, how should the tasks be rearranged?
• How accurate were the original estimates of time needed to complete the various tasks? If estimates were inaccurate, what factors should be considered in the next planning cycle?
• Were the appropriate individuals assigned to the tasks and did they have adequate skills and time to complete the tasks effectively? How can

task assignments be improved for the next planning cycle?

APPROPRIATENESS OF THE LEVELS OF EFFORT

Important decisions were made during the planning process regarding levels of effort in each of the planning phases. A review of these intended levels of effort should consider:

• Did the library work at the level of effort that was originally intended? Why did any variance occur?
• Would different levels of effort for particular planning steps have been more appropriate than those selected? If yes, why?
• What levels of effort should be given to planning steps in the next planning cycle?

COMMUNICATION

An important ingredient for the success of the planning process is the degree to which participants communicated effectively with each other. A review of written planning material can offer some indicators of the success of written communication. But the key factor is the effectiveness of interpersonal communication among planning participants, specifically:

- To what degree were group processes effective? Were written agendas and minutes of meetings maintained?
- What factors contributed to or limited effective communication between and among the various planning participants, for example, between the library staff and library management?
- Were planning participants able to obtain the necessary planning information, for example, data from Looking Around, when needed? If not, why not?
- To what degree were local government officials appropriately informed throughout the planning process?
- Were news releases adequate and well-timed? If not, why not?
- What actions can be taken to improve communication processes?

OTHER FACTORS

When reviewing information on the above topics, additional factors may be identified that affected the success with which the process of planning was completed. For example, the organizational structure of the library, the involvement of state library or other consultants, or unexpected "crises" may have helped or hindered planning efforts. As such factors are identified, they should be considered in assessing the overall process.

Discussions and Surveys

A second method of reviewing the process of planning is discussions and/or surveys with individuals who participated in the process. Not all libraries would do this, only those that have committed a moderate or extensive level of effort to Reviewing Results.

However, this aspect of the review can be especially useful. It can provide additional recommendations and assess the accuracy of other review information. Topics may focus on areas or planning steps that may have been most difficult to complete, those that were least understood, or those that produced unexpected results. Possible topics include:

- How did involvement in the planning process affect the staff's ability to complete regular responsibilities?
- Are there specific suggestions for streamlining or making more effective specific steps, for example, setting objectives?
- Is there a need to develop additional skills/ competencies related to the planning process?
- To what degree did staff see results and changes

occur from their involvement in the planning process?
- What factors contributed most to the success or to problems experienced during the planning process?
- What is the staff's attitude toward the next planning cycle, for example, eagerness, skepticism, reservations, etc.

One approach to obtaining this input is to meet informally with planning participants. It can take the form of one-to-one meetings (reviewer with participant), group meetings with library departments or individual branches, or "open forums" on a particular aspect of the planning process.

Different planning participants may have different perspectives on the planning process. Thus, topics to be covered and the specific questions to be asked should be targeted to the information or involvement of those who participated in the planning process. Results and recommendations from the discussions can be summarized on Workform Q (see Figure 34).

Another approach is to conduct one or more surveys. The surveys can be of two basic types: broad, i.e., covering many aspects of the planning process, or narrow, i.e., covering one particular aspect of the planning process. The type that might be selected depends on:

- The topics on which comment is desired
- The amount of time that can be spent on conducting such surveys
- The degree to which it is believed that such surveys will augment or validate other review information.

The last factor may be especially important. Reviews of the success of the planning cycle based on the views of only one or two individuals may fail to consider adequately the views of others who may also have been directly involved in the planning process.

Step 4: Recycle the Information

In this final step, those involved in the review take what has been learned and offer recommendations to assist the next planning committee improve the planning cycle. At this stage, there has been either an informal discussion of factors related to the success of the plan and the planning process, or, there are a number of completed workforms (L, M, N, O, P, and Q) that assess the success of the plan and the planning process.

This step prepares the library for beginning the next planning cycle, links current planning activities to the next cycle, and encourages a smooth transition from one planning cycle to the next. Much of the work has already been done to complete this step.

Organizing for Recycling

An important decision to make before starting the recycling process is: who will have responsibility for Planning to Plan in the next planning cycle. Thus, if a planning committee is to plan for the next planning cycle (as described in Chapter 2), then that committee should be established and involved in the recycling process.

If the library director prefers to have a planning officer prepare for the next planning cycle, that person can be actively involved in recycling. Overlap among those involved in the recycling process and those preparing for the next planning cycle is likely to improve the next planning cycle.

Summarizing Recommendations

As a result of completing the review, the director or the planning committee has assessed the topics and workforms described earlier in this chapter. Discussions of these topics and workforms can be held among the director, planning committee members, and library staff to consider the feasibility of the recommendations.

The library director takes an active role in these discussions and provides a managerial perspective on the recommendations. After these discussions, the director or planning committee prepares final recommendations to improve the next planning cycle. Workform R, Recommendations for the Next Planning Cycle (see Figure 35), suggests one way for organizing these recommendations and linking them to their appropriate place in the planning process.

Included in Workform R (see Figure 35) is a category of recommendations regarding the review. The director or the planning committee can complete this section after the reviewing process. It offers an opportunity to assess how well the review was accomplished and to make recommendations for improving the review during the next planning cycle. Questions to consider here include:

- Did the information from the review identify specific areas of the planning process that could be improved? If not, why not?

- Was the amount of information obtained worth the time and resources committed to the review process? If not, why not?
- Was the review process well-organized and conducted effectively within a given time schedule?
- Should additional reporting and/or record keeping mechanisms be maintained during the planning process to assist in the next review?
- What additional factors should be reviewed during the next planning cycle that were not reviewed this time?

Integrating Recommendations

The recommendations from Workform R (see Figure 35) represent the primary means that information learned from the review is incorporated into the next planning process. But integrating the recommendations means that those charged with the responsibility for the next planning cycle carefully consider them when the library begins the next Planning to Plan. Such integration will be enhanced by the director:

- Distributing a copy of the recommendations listed in Workform R (see Figure 35) to the members of the planning committee for the next planning cycle
- Asking planning participants from the current planning process to share their views on the cycle's successes and difficulties with the new planning committee
- Making a short presentation to the new planning committee summarizing the recommendations from the previous planning committee
- Incorporating appropriate recommendations into the new Planning to Plan documents, e.g., the budget and planning chart.

Throughout this process it is important for the library director to be actively involved in the review and to act upon the recommendations in the next Planning to Plan.

Excellence through Planning

The end of the recycling process connects into Planning to Plan for the next planning cycle. The two phases, in reality, merge together as the library moves from the end of one planning cycle to the beginning of the next. The ongoing nature of the planning process is an opportunity for library planners to learn from their experi-

WORKFORM R   Recommendations for the Next Planning Cycle

A. Planning to Plan

   Recommendations: _____

   _____

   _____

   _____

   _____

B. Looking Around

   Recommendations: _____

   _____

   _____

   _____

   _____

C. Roles and Mission

   Recommendations: _____

   _____

   _____

   _____

   _____

D. Goals and Objectives

   Recommendations: _____

   _____

   _____

   _____

   _____

E. Taking Action

   Recommendations: _____

   _____

   _____

   _____

   _____

F. The Planning Document

   Recommendations: _____

   _____

   _____

   _____

   _____

G. Review

   Recommendations: _____

   _____

   _____

   _____

   _____

H. Overall Recommendations (those that cut across the various steps, not specifically covered above):

   _____

   _____

   _____

   _____

   _____

FIGURE 35   Reduced Workform R: Recommendations for the Next Planning Cycle

ence with the planning process and incorporate that learning into the next cycle.

Incorporating these recommendations into succeeding planning cycles provides a sound and continuing managerial basis for effective public library services. Each repetition of the planning cycle will assist librarians to better meet the library and information needs of the community and serve as the fabric that ties together local community information services. Further, each new planning cycle will increase the quality of the planning process and the degree to which public libraries are managed effectively.

Completing a planning process such as that described here is an important and significant accomplishment for your library. Congratulations! You can take pride in the fact that your library services are based on a formalized planning process. Library services will continue to improve and better meet community information needs. Your library is prepared to face the challenges of the future.

Sources for Additional Information

Anthony, William P. *Practical Strategic Planning: A Guide and Manual for Line Managers.* Westport, Conn.: Greenwood Press, 1985.

   Chapter 14, Systems for Corrective Action, offers a number of suggestions for fine-tuning the planning process. These suggestions are especially appropriate to consider during the review and recycling process.

Riggs, Donald E. *Strategic Planning for Library Managers.* Phoenix, Ariz.: Oryx Press, 1984.

   Pages 113—115 provide a useful questionnaire, "How Effective Is Your Library's Strategic Planning System." Some of the questions on this form may be incorporated in Steps 2 and 3 of this chapter.

Appendix A
Summary of Measures from <u>Output</u> <u>Measures for Public Libraries</u>*

Browsers' Fill Rate
Definition: Proportion of browsing searches that are successful.

Calculation: NUMBER OF BROWSERS FINDING SOMETHING divided by NUMBER OF BROWSERS.

Data Collection: Materials Availability Survey, a survey of library users.

Circulation per Capita
Definition: Average annual circulation per person in the community served.

Calculation: ANNUAL CIRCULATION divided by POPULATION OF LEGAL SERVICE AREA.

Data Collection: Most libraries already count circulation.

Document Delivery
Definition: Percent of requests available within 7, 14, and 30 days or longer.

Data Collection: Track one month's worth of requests for up to 30 days.

In-Library Materials Use per Capita
Definition: Number of materials used in the library per person served.

Calculation: ANNUAL IN-LIBRARY MATERIALS USE divided by POPULATION OF LEGAL SERVICE AREA.

Data Collection: Ask users not to reshelve, and for one week count all materials used.

Library Visits per Capita
Definition: Number of library visits during the year per person in the community served.

Calculation: ANNUAL NUMBER OF LIBRARY VISITS divided by POPULATION OF LEGAL SERVICE AREA.

Data Collection: Turnstile counter, or count people entering the building during one week.

Program Attendance per Capita
Definition: Program attendance per person in the population served.

Calculation: ANNUAL PROGRAM ATTENDANCE divided by the POPULATION OF LEGAL SERVICE AREA.

Data Collection: Count the audience at all programs during the entire year.

Reference Completion Rate
Definition: Proportion of reference transactions successfully completed, in judgment of librarian.

Calculation: NUMBER OF REFERENCE TRANSACTIONS COMPLETED divided by NUMBER OF REFERENCE TRANSACTIONS.

Data Collection: Reference staff tallies sample of reference transactions.

Reference Transactions per Capita
Definition: Number of reference transactions per person in the community served.

Calculation: ANNUAL NUMBER OF REFERENCE TRANSACTIONS divided by POPULATION OF LEGAL SERVICE AREA.

---

*Nancy A. Van House, Mary Jo Lynch, Charles R. McClure, Douglas L. Zweizig, and Eleanor J. Rodger, *Output Measures for Public Libraries,* second edition (Chicago: American Library Association, 1987).

Data Collection: If the library does not already count reference transactions, reference staff tallies questions during a one-week sample period.

Registrations as a Percentage of the Population

Definition: Proportion of the people in the community served who have registered as library users.

Calculation: LIBRARY REGISTRATIONS divided by POPULATION OF LEGAL SERVICE AREA.

Data Collection: Count number of registrations in library registration file.

Subject and Author Fill Rate

Definition: Proportion of subject and author searches that are successful.

Calculation: NUMBER OF SUBJECTS AND AUTHORS FOUND divided by NUMBER OF SUBJECTS AND AUTHORS SOUGHT.

Data Collection: Materials Availability Survey, a survey of library users.

Title Fill Rate

Definition: Proportion of title searches that are successful.

Calculation: NUMBER OF TITLES FOUND divided by NUMBER OF TITLES SOUGHT.

Data Collection: Materials Availability Survey, a survey of library users.

Turnover Rate

Definition: Average circulation per volume owned.

Calculation: ANNUAL CIRCULATION divided by the library's HOLDINGS.

Data Collection: Use existing data, or estimate collection size by measuring shelflist.

Appendix B
Planning and Role Setting Workforms

The workforms presented on the following pages are intended to assist librarians complete the planning and role setting process. A number of these workforms can be duplicated directly from these pages. Others, however, provide only a general outline for the format and content of the workform. These may require additional content, redesign, or reformatting before use.

WORKFORM A Simple Planning Budget

Budget Category	Projected Expenditure
Planning Committee: (Consider number of meetings, travel and food costs)	_____
Consultants: (Consider desired scope of consultant activities)	_____
Data Collection: (Consider level of effort for Looking Around)	_____
General Costs:	
Copying	_____
Printing	_____
Extra telephone charges	_____
Extra postage charges	_____
Additional staff support	_____
Total:	_____

WORKFORM B Planning Chart

Task	Person	Month											
		1	2	3	4	5	6	7	8	9	10	11	12
1.													
2.													
3.													
4.													
5.													
6.													
7.													
8.													
9.													
10.													
11.													
12.													

Notes and Explanations:

WORKFORM C, Part A Options for Library Planning Information

COMMUNITY CHARACTERISTICS

Information on Individuals	Current/Local	Comparative
Percentage of population under 5 years of age	_____	_____
Percentage of population 5 to 17 years of age	_____	_____
Percentage of population 17 to 65 years of age	_____	_____
Percentage of population over 65 years of age	_____	_____
Per capita personal income	_____	_____
Percentage of persons below poverty level	_____	_____
Percentage of population over 25 with		
12 or more years of school completed	_____	_____
16 or more years of school completed	_____	_____

Other: (Cite other statistics, describe trends or characteristics)

_____ _____ _____

_____ _____ _____

_____ _____ _____

Information on Families and Households		
Total number of households	_____	_____
Average number of persons per household	_____	_____
Total number of families	_____	_____
Total number of nonfamily households	_____	_____
Total number of one-person households	_____	_____
Median family income	_____	_____
Percentage of families below poverty line	_____	_____

Racial/language/ethnic groups: (List appropriate groups and percentages for your community.)

_____

_____

_____

Other: (Cite other statistics, describe trends or characteristics)

_____ _____ _____

_____ _____ _____

_____ _____ _____

WORKFORM C, Part B Options for Library Planning Information (continued)

Information on the Community	Current/Local	Comparative
Total population of legal service area (See *OMPL*, second edition)	_____	_____
Assessed Valuation per Capita	_____	_____
Percentage of labor force in manufacturing	_____	_____
Percentage of labor force in wholesale and related services	_____	_____
Percentage of labor force in professional and related groups	_____	_____
Percentage of labor force in government	_____	_____
Percentage of labor force self-employed	_____	_____
Percentage of labor force in other locally significant industry (Specify:)		
_____	_____	_____
Unemployment rate	_____	_____
Number of religious groups or organizations	_____	_____
Number of schools	_____	_____
Elementary	_____	_____
Secondary	_____	_____
High School	_____	_____
Vocational/technical	_____	_____
Colleges/universities	_____	_____
Number of hospitals	_____	_____

Other libraries, information providers, museums, or recreational facilties (List or give the total number for each category)

_____

_____

	Current/Local	Comparative
Number of newspapers	_____	_____
Number of radio and television stations	_____	_____

Types and number of clubs and organizations

_____

_____

Other: (Cite other statistics, describe trends or characteristics)

_____	_____	_____
_____	_____	_____
_____	_____	_____

WORKFORM C, Part C   Options for Library Planning Information (continued)

LIBRARY CHARACTERISTICS

<u>Collection</u>   Current/Local   Comparative

    Number of volumes   _____   _____

    Formats available (List)

    Other: (Comment on collection scope, currency, subject strengths, etc.)

<u>Staff</u>:

    Total number of employees   _____   _____

    Total number of full-time equivalent employees   _____   _____

    Number of professional employees   _____   _____

    Number of paraprofessional employees   _____   _____

    Number of clerical employees   _____   _____

    Number of maintenance workers   _____   _____

    Other: (Describe any other important staff characteristics)

<u>Financial Resources</u>:

    Total operating budget   _____   _____

    Expenditures per capita   _____   _____

<u>Facilities</u>:

    Number of service outlets   _____   _____

    Total hours of service per week at all service outlets   _____   _____

    Total number of square feet at all service outlets   _____   _____

    Total seating capacity at all service outlets   _____   _____

    Number of meeting rooms at all service outlets   _____   _____

    Equipment available for public use (list)

    Other: (Describe any other important features such as layout, parking, accessibility, etc.)

WORKFORM C, Part D   Options for Library Planning Information (continued)

Output Measures (See *OMPL*, second edition)	Current/Local	Comparative
Browsers' Fill Rate	⎯⎯	⎯⎯
Circulation per Capita	⎯⎯	⎯⎯
Document Delivery	⎯⎯	⎯⎯
In-Library Materials Use per Capita	⎯⎯	⎯⎯
Library Visits per Capita	⎯⎯	⎯⎯
Program Attendance per Capita	⎯⎯	⎯⎯
Reference Completion Rate	⎯⎯	⎯⎯
Reference Transactions per Capita	⎯⎯	⎯⎯
Registrations as a Percentage of the Population	⎯⎯	⎯⎯
Subject and Author Fill Rate	⎯⎯	⎯⎯
Title Fill Rate	⎯⎯	⎯⎯
Turnover Rate	⎯⎯	⎯⎯
Other: (Specify any other relevant measures)		
_____	⎯⎯	⎯⎯
_____	⎯⎯	⎯⎯
_____	⎯⎯	⎯⎯
_____	⎯⎯	⎯⎯
_____	⎯⎯	⎯⎯
_____	⎯⎯	⎯⎯

WORKFORM D   Translating the Findings of Looking Around

Major Finding	Impact on Library Roles and Services?	Opportunities?	Possible Library Responses?
1.			
2.			
3.			
etc.			

WORKFORM E   Selecting Library Roles Worksheet

_____
(Group)

In the columns below, please allocate 100 points. You need not divide points equally, and some roles may receive no points. Note that 20 of the 100 points have already been assigned to cover basic library activities and roles not selected for emphasis. In the first column, distribute the 80 remaining points based on how you see *current* library activities being directed. In the second column, distribute the 80 points the way you feel library activities *should* be directed.

Role	Current Activities	Desired Commitment
Community Activities Center		
Community Information Center		
Formal Education Support Center		
Independent Learning Center		
Popular Materials Library		
Preschoolers' Door to Learning		
Reference Library		
Research Center		
Miscellaneous Activities and Roles Not Selected for Emphasis	20	20
Total	100	100

WORKFORM F   Drafting the Mission Statement

Most mission statements have common elements. In the space below, jot down a few sentences or phrases that capture your understanding of the library's mission for the role(s) indicated and your personal perspective. Check whether the role designated is a primary or secondary role for your library.

Role: _____   Primary Role: _____

Secondary Role: _____

Mission Statement Elements

Who:
Needs:
Concepts:

Who: People in the community, children, young adults, seniors, families, library users, library nonusers, students, independent learners, ethnic groups, the institutionalized, etc.

Needs: Recreational, leisure, informational, educational, cultural, social, historic, civic, intellectual, etc.

Concepts: Access to information, meeting users' needs, reaching new users, reaching nonusers, interlibrary cooperation, intellectual freedom, public awareness of library services, linking people with ideas, stimulating intellectual life, preserving cultural and intellectual heritage, helping individuals solve daily practical problems, etc.

WORKFORM G Assessing the Measurability of an Objective

Objective 1: _____

_____

_____

1. What is the measure for this objective? _____

_____

2. What data will be needed for the measure? _____

_____

3. What are the procedures for obtaining the data? _____

_____

_____

4. How easily can these procedures be implemented and the data obtained?

_____

_____

5. To what degree are adequate staff time and other resources present to collect and analyze the data?

_____

_____

Objective 2: _____

_____

_____

. . . repeat questions 1—5 above, and continue for each objective.

NOTE: If responses for each of the questions on this workform cannot be provided, the objective should be revised or abandoned.

WORKFORM H Ranking Objectives

Instructions: Please indicate your assessment of the overall importance of each objective listed below. Write in the right-hand column the number that represents your assessment of that objective based on the following code:

5 = Essential: Must Be Done! Find   3 = Important: Should Be Done If   1 = Desirable: Do If Time and
     a Way of Funding   Possible   Funds Allow.

Objective and Rationale	Rank

Objective 1: _____   _____

_____

_____

   [Rationale If Available] _____

_____

_____

_____

Objective 2: _____   _____

_____

_____

   [Rationale If Available] _____

_____

_____

_____

Objective 3: _____   _____

_____

_____

   [Rationale If Available] _____

_____

_____

WORKFORM I, Part A   Summary of Roles, Goals, and Objectives for Library without Multiple Outlets

Primary Library Roles: Level of Commitment: 50%

     Role 1: _____

     Role 2: _____

Secondary Library Roles: Level of Commitment: 30%

     Role 3: _____

     Role 4: _____

Remainder of Library Roles and Activities   Level of Commitment: 20%
100%

Mission Statement: _____

_____

_____

_____

Goal 1: _____

_____

     Objective 1.1: _____

     _____

     Objective 1.2: _____

     _____

Goal 2: _____

_____

     Objective 2.1: _____

     _____

     Objective 2.2: _____

     _____

NOTE: The library should list the appropriate number of goals and objectives as agreed upon from the ranking process (see Workform H).

WORKFORM I, Part B Summary of Roles, Goals, and Objectives for Library with Multiple Outlets
(Assuming the planning committee has agreed that branches have branch roles, goals, and objectives.)

Branch Name: _____ Date _____

Mission Statement for the Library: _____

_____

_____

_____

Primary Library Roles: Level of Commitment: 50%

    Role 1: _____

    Role 2: _____

Secondary Library Roles: Level of Commitment: 30%

    Role 3: _____

    Role 4: _____

Remainder of Library Roles and Activities   Level of Commitment: 20%
                                                                     _____
                                                                     100%

Branch Goal 1: _____

_____

    Objective 1.1: _____

    _____

    Objective 1.2: _____

    _____

Branch Goal 2: _____

_____

    Objective 2.1: _____ . . . and so forth

NOTE: The library should list the appropriate number of goals and objectives as agreed upon from the ranking process
(see Workform H).

WORKFORM J Listing Activities

Objective #_____: Objective Statement: _____

Name	Brief Description
Possible Activity #1	
Possible Activity #2	
Possible Activity #3	

Notes: _____

WORKFORM K Activities Status Report

Person Reporting: _____ Date: _____

Objective: _____

_____

Activity Name: _____

_____

Tasks: (If available, append completed Planning Charts, Workform B).

Current Status on implementing tasks:

1. Are the tasks being implemented on schedule?

2. Are adequate resources/equipment available?

3. Have any problems been encountered with implementing the tasks?

4. Are revisions needed for the tasks or for the planning chart? If yes, please detail:

Comments/Suggestions from Director or Planning Committee:

NOTE: To be used for moderate or extensive level of effort only.

WORKFORM L   Assessment of Activities and Objectives

A.   Objective # : _____

B.   Activity(ies) used to accomplish this objective: _____

C.   Strengths and weaknesses of the activity(ies): _____

D.   Recommendations to improve these activities: _____

E.   Evidence of the degree to which the objective was accomplished: _____

F.   Factors that contributed to or hindered the accomplishment of the objectives:

G.   Additional information needed from a "Supplemental Looking Around" regarding this objective prior to the next objectives cycle.

H.   Recommendations for this objective for the next objectives cycle:

WORKFORM M   Review of Goals

Goal Statement: _____

_____

_____

A. How did this goal assist in fulfilling the library's mission?

_____

_____

_____

B. To what degree did this goal enable the library to fulfill its roles? Which roles, specifically, does this goal address?

_____

_____

_____

C. How did this goal support or compete with other goals?

_____

_____

_____

D. To what extent did this goal provide a basis from which library staff could write clear and measurable objectives?

_____

_____

_____

E .Recommendations for revising this goal statement:
   [ ] maintain the goal as currently written
   [ ] drop this goal
   [ ] revise this goal in the following manner: _____

_____

_____

_____

WORKFORM N   Review of Roles

Role Name: _____ Level of Commitment: _____

A. Adequacy of critical resources to fulfill this role:

_____

_____

_____

_____

_____

B. Indicators of fulfilling this role (include appropriate output measures):

_____

_____

_____

_____

_____

C. Changes in library or community conditions that affected or may affect this role:

_____

_____

_____

_____

_____

D. Recommendations for changing the role or its level of commitment:

_____

_____

_____

_____

_____

WORKFORM O Review of Mission Statement

Existing Mission Statement: _____

_____

_____

_____

_____

_____

A. Significant changes since last planning cycle that may affect the mission statement.

1. _____

2. _____

3. _____

4. _____

B. Aspects of the existing mission statement that are still appropriate:

_____

_____

_____

_____

C. Aspects of the existing mission statement that are no longer appropriate or need to be changed:

_____

_____

_____

_____

D. Recommended changes in wording the existing mission statement:

_____

_____

_____

_____

WORKFORM P   Review of Information Gathered by Looking Around

*A.   Data summary form or data collection activity: _____

_____

1.   Information especially useful: _____

_____

2.   Information not especially useful: _____

_____

3.   Information needed for next data collection activity: _____

_____

_____

B.   Data summary form or data collection activity: _____

_____

. . . and so forth for each data summary form or data collection activity used.

Recommendations for the Next Looking Around:

1.   Information and data collection activities to be added:

_____

_____

_____

2.   Information and data collection activities to be eliminated:

_____

_____

_____

3.   Procedures by which the process of Looking Around can be improved:

_____

_____

_____

*The data summary forms or data collection activities referred to in parts A and B are those used in Chapter 3. If the form is to be distributed to planning committee members or library staff, fill in the name of the data summary form or data collection activity prior to distribution.

WORKFORM Q Summary Workform to Review Planning Process

A. Review of Library Records

1. Budget

Summary Comments: _____

_____

Recommendations: _____

_____

_____

2. Staff Time

Summary Comments: _____

_____

Recommendations: _____

_____

_____

3. Planning Participants' Roles

Summary Comments: _____

_____

Recommendations: _____

_____

_____

4. The Planning Schedule

Summary Comments: _____

_____

Recommendations: _____

_____

_____

WORKFORM Q Summary Workform to Review Planning Process (continued)

5. Levels of Effort

   Summary Comments: _____

   _____

   Recommendations: _____

   _____

   _____

6. Internal Communication

   Summary Comments: _____

   _____

   Recommendations: _____

   _____

   _____

7. Other Factors

   Summary Comments: _____

   _____

   Recommendations: _____

   _____

   _____

B. Discussions and Surveys

   Summary Comments: _____

   _____

   _____

   Recommendations: _____

   _____

   _____

WORKFORM R Recommendations for the Next Planning Cycle

A. Planning to Plan

Recommendations: _____

_____

_____

_____

_____

B. Looking Around

Recommendations: _____

_____

_____

_____

_____

C. Roles and Mission

Recommendations: _____

_____

_____

_____

_____

D. Goals and Objectives

Recommendations: _____

_____

_____

_____

_____

_____

WORKFORM R   Recommendations for the Next Planning Cycle (continued)

E.   Taking Action

Recommendations: _____

_____

_____

_____

_____

F.   The Planning Document

Recommendations: _____

_____

_____

_____

_____

G.   Review

Recommendations: _____

_____

_____

_____

H.   Overall Recommendations (those that cut across the various steps, not specifically covered above):

_____

_____

_____

_____

_____

_____

Biographical Information about the Authors

Charles R. McClure completed his PhD at Rutgers University. He is President of Information Management Consultant Services, Inc., and Professor at the School of Information Studies, Syracuse University, Syracuse, N.Y. He has served as principal investigator on a number of funded projects, including the Public Library Development Project, and works as a management consultant to public, academic, corporate, and state libraries. He is the author or co-author of: *Planning for Library Services* (New York: Haworth Press, 1982); *Strategies for Library Administration* (Littleton, Colo.: Libraries Unlimited, 1982); *Research for Decision Making* (Chicago: American Library Association, 1984); *Output Measures for Public Libraries,* second edition (Chicago: American Library Association, 1987), and a number of other articles and monographs.

Amy Owen received her BA in Humanities and an MLS from Brigham Young University. Since 1981 she has served as Deputy Director at the Utah State Library, Salt Lake City, where she has oversight responsibility for library development and long-range planning. Her planning experience includes participation on the Governor's Utah Systems Planning Team, development of the *Utah Plan for Library and Information Services,* and consulting and workshops on various planning topics. Most recently, she has worked with the Utah Advisory Committee to produce *The Upgrade Process: Planning, Evaluating and Measuring for Public Library Excellence* (Salt Lake City: Utah State Library, 1987). She has also been an active member in a number of professional associations.

Douglas L. Zweizig completed his PhD at Syracuse University. Currently he is Professor at the School of Library and Information Studies, University of Wisconsin–Madison. He previously held the position of Senior Research Associate at King Research, Inc. He has written numerous articles related to planning and performance measures. He is co-author of both the first and second editions of *Output Measures for Public Libraries* (Chicago: American Library Association, 1982 and 1987). He has been a consultant to various libraries and most recently, with Karen Krueger, has completed the report *Standards for Public Library Services in Ohio* (Columbus, Ohio: State Library of Ohio, 1986).

Mary Jo Lynch completed her PhD at Rutgers University. Since 1978 she has held the position of Director of the Office for Research at the American Library Association. She has worked as a reference librarian in academic libraries, has taught in three different library education programs, and has been a frequent contributor to the professional literature. She served as Project Coordinator for the work that led to publication of *A Planning Process for Public Libraries* (Chicago: American Library Association, 1980), and also served on the Steering Committee that guided the development of the first edition of *Output Measures for Public Libraries* (Chicago: American Library Association, 1982). She has completed several projects in the area of library statistics under contract to the U.S. Department of Education. Most recently she directed a pilot project to coordinate data collection done in the state library agencies and served as co-author for *Output Measures for Public Libraries,* second edition (Chicago: American Library Association, 1987).

Nancy A. Van House completed her PhD at the School of Library and Information Studies, University of California, Berkeley, where she is currently Associate Professor. Before her appointment at Berkeley she served as a Senior Research Associate at King Research, Inc. She is the author of numerous books and articles including *Public Library User Fees* (Westport, Conn.: Greenwood Press, 1983) and co-author (under the name DeWath) of *A Planning Process for Public Libraries* (Chicago: American Library Association, 1980). She is also the co-author of *Output Measures for Public Libraries,* second edition (Chicago: American Library Association, 1987). She does research and consulting on library planning and evaluation, the economics of library services, and the library labor market.

Index

Prepared by Answers Unlimited, Inc.